D1171026

PAYDAY
EVERYDAY

Robert G. Lee

PAYDAY EVERYDAY

"The Incomparable Memoirs of a Pulpit Giant"...
The Editors

**BROADMAN PRESS/
NASHVILLE, TENNESSEE**

© Copyright 1974 • Broadman Press
All rights reserved
ISBN: 0-8054-5548-5
4255-48

Library of Congress Catalog Card Number: 74-80721
Dewey Decimal Classification: B
Printed in the United States of America

PREFACE

The late Robert Greene Lee requires no introduction. This preacher of the gospel is known and loved throughout the nation—and around the world.

He has been called "a legend in his time," "a pulpit giant," "the king of preachers," and a "preacher's preacher." In *Payday Everyday* we have "the incomparable memoirs of a pulpit giant."

Dr. Lee was recognized for his powerful, convincing pulpit oratory, his unparalleled grasp of the English language, his ability to keep a congregation spellbound, his uncanny understanding of human nature, his spiritual depth, his compassionate shepherd's heart . . . words fail to do justice to Dr. Lee and his amazing ministry.

Dr. Lee would have no part of having his virtues extolled. As always he wants his Lord to receive all glory and honor.

Here was a man who had hobnobbed with princes and kings, but was equally at home with all human beings. One of our Broadman editors watched the following happen. Dr. Lee heard that a little boy was having a birthday. Immediately Dr. Lee asked the boy, "Son, would you like a picture of Abraham Lincoln?" The boy, somewhat puzzled, replied, "Yes sir." Dr. Lee reached into his billfold and then handed the boy a five-dollar bill—which does contain a picture of Lincoln. Dr. Lee has never been too busy for people.

Yet, here was a man who hated sin with the same intensity that he loved the Lord and people. Throughout his lengthy ministry he cried out against evil in every form and wherever it exists. As a pastor Dr. Lee was second to none in his care of the flock. At Bellevue

Baptist Church, where he served from 1927 to 1960, he memorized every name on the church roll, and Bellevue was and is one of the largest churches in the world.

Here for the first time are his memoirs—autobiographical glimpses into the life and times of the preacher who is often called "the greatest preacher in the twentieth century" and "one of the greatest preachers in the history of Christianity." His memoirs give considerable insight into the massive heart of this man. Dr. Lee was an author that was probably called on to write more forewords to more books than any one man in Christendom. Yet, he really needed no one to write his.

When the Lord called Dr. Lee home, the ninety-two-year-old preacher was still praising God.

What else can we say? Dr. Lee was truly a legend, a pulpit giant, an institution within himself. His memoirs are shared for entertainment, true. And to provide a chuckle here and there. And to encourage the reader in the Christian walk. But most of all to glorify Jesus Christ.

So, laugh and live with this saint of God, Robert Greene Lee. Read from his pen incomparable slices of life. Rejoice in an unforgettable experience.

THE EDITORS

CONTENTS

INTRODUCTION

Many times in recent years I have been asked how old I am. Well, I am as old as Coca-Cola. This drink, advertised as "the pause that refreshes," was concocted and sold and drunk first in 1886—the year I was born.

At eighty-eight, I am eleven years older than George W. Truett who died at seventy-seven after being pastor of the First Baptist Church of Dallas for nearly fifty years.

I am thirteen years older than Lee Scarborough who, after serving many years as president of Southwestern Baptist Theological Seminary, died at seventy-five years of age.

I am fourteen years older than M. E. Dodd who, after serving many years as pastor of the First Baptist Church of Shreveport, died at age seventy-four.

I am thirty-five years older than was Napoleon who died at age fifty-two "a chained Prometheus, the world exultant at his fall." I am eleven years older than Robert Browning, the great poet, who died at seventy-seven.

I am five years older than was Lord Tennyson who died at eighty-three. I am three years younger than was Winston Churchill who died at ninety-one years of age. About him, President Dwight Eisenhower wrote: "Neither England nor the world shall soon look upon his like again."

I am fifty-one years older than Lord Byron who died at thirty-six, and two years younger than was Gladstone who died at eighty-nine. Concerning Gladstone, his biographer wrote:

> In Christ his mighty intellect found anchorage;
> In Christ his impetuous temper found restraint;
> In Christ his versatile personality found fulfillment.

Once I spoke to Thomas Edison, the great inventor, and to Henry Ford, the auto manufacturer. Both died younger than I now am.

Charles Dickens, author superlative, died at fifty-eight

Keats died at twenty-six.

Shelly died at thirty.

Edgar Allen Poe died at forty.

Queen Victoria died in 1901 at eighty-two.

All the presidents of the United States died younger than I am.

But, after all, it is not how *long* people live, but how *much* they live that matters most. Life is not measured or evaluated by birth-dates but by deeds.

> We live in deeds, not years,
> In thoughts, not breaths,
> In feelings, not in figures on a dial.
> We should count time by heartthrobs.
> He lives longest who lives the noblest,
> Acts the best—
> Lives more in weeks than in years
> Do some whose fat blood sleeps
> As it creeps along their veins.

Robert Greene Lee

1.
"Some Heaven Here"

Birthplace and Springs' Mansion

I think often of the little log cabin where my birth cries were heard—and where, so she said, my mother's first prayer for me was that I would grow up to be a preacher.

In this cabin on a poor farm where "Aunt Harriet," a black woman, a sort of expert midwife, took my baby body, fresh from my mother's womb, in her black hands, did some sort of dance scross the plank floor and said: "Praise God! God done sont a preacher to dis here house. Yaas suh! Yaas ma'am!"

My father was a sharecropper. Frank Massey furnished the dwelling house, the land for farming, the mules for plowing, the wagon for hauling, and tools necessary for work of all kinds.

My dad gave Mr. Massey, the owner, one bushel of corn out oī two, one bale of cotton out of two bales, one basket of fruit out of two baskets—well, one half of all he produced. Out of the half my dad received for his labors, he furnished food, clothes, and all things possible, though not all things necessary, for a growing family.

From this poor little farm where my father was a sharecropper, we moved to the beautifully stately and stately beautiful Springs' Mansion, five miles away, built by slave work and finished in 1804.

Here my father, at a salary of forty dollars per month and with the mansion for a house for his family, was superintendent of the farm and the cultivation thereof.

When as a little boy wearing a dress (as was the custom for little boys in those days) I walked with my mother between the white columns into the large hall of the mansion, I thought I was entering heaven. I asked her: "Is this heaven?"

"No honey," she answered, "but we can so live and love that we can have some heaven here."

Originally, this glorious home had nineteen rooms. Two of them and a library room, Mr. Eli Springs reserved to himself for any visit he saw fit to make.

A spiral stair that led from downstairs to the upstairs had a sharp curve in the railing. I slid down this many times. Seldom did I walk down this stairway. In the attic above the second floor, I once saw some Confederate uniforms, some old trunks, an ante-bellum spinning wheel, some scythes and some discarded old furniture which today would be the delight of dealers in antiques.

Outside the house was a well with a windlass and old wooden bucket. Near this well was a crude little stone house, fifteen by fifteen, with heavy wooden doors, big locks, and two iron-barred windows— used in slave days for punishment of disobedient slaves. Under the first floor of the mansion, in the rear, were rooms where the house slaves once had quarters.

In front of the mansion was a big lawn surrounded by a high picket fence painted white. The lawn was shaded by some huge oak and magnolia trees. On this lawn, once, as an eight-year-old lad, I saw my father with ferocious anger demand of the owner of the farm and mansion that he leave the lawn—together with two score folks who were having a dance in the hall of the mansion.

My father, riding up to the front gate of the lawn on old Bob, the saddle horse, dropped the bridle reins around the gate post, took off his straw hat, and walked toward Mr. Springs who was playing cards with some ladies at a table on which was a bottle of rye whiskey and wine glasses.

My father, taking no notice of the ladies, walked up to the table and said: "Eli, I give you twenty minutes to get this dancing crowd out of the house and this card-playing, liquor-drinking crowd off this lawn. If you don't *get* it off, I'll *put* you off!" With a family to raise, I'm not going to have such devil-doings around here!"

Mr. Springs, his breath warm with the smell of whiskey, gave orders to the orchestra in the hall to quit playing, and said: "We must all go now." As a lad, I was impressed by the quickness with which the orchestra stopped playing and especially with the way in which the black man with the big bass viol left the house. In less than twenty minutes all the tables were vacant as to those playing cards and drinking rye whiskey. When all had gone, Dad quieted down and went in to eat the noonday meal. I think I never saw such a manifestation of anger in all my life. Maybe Jesus, who cleansed the Temple in Jerusalem, would have done as did my dad.

Think now of

A Farm Bought

After living six years in the Springs' Mansion, my father bought from a Dr. Kilpatrick, a farm of one hundred and eighty-eight acres— promising to pay for it, "so much a year," within ten years. This farm on the Dobey's Bridge Road, three miles from Fort Mill, South Carolina, was very hilly with fields of red clay and white sand. It was said by some to be so poor that a man "could hardly raise an umbrella on it, much less the mortgage!"

The house had five rooms with a hall, two chimneys, and four fireplaces and a chimney flue for the kitchen. It had a small back porch and front porch—clear across the front of the house. There was a deep well in the backyard near a corncrib which was near the barn. About a hundred yards from the house was a cow barn where the cows were fed, milked, and sheltered.

On the back porch, with no screens, was a nail on which hung a big towel which was used to wipe the face and hands after washing in the tin bowl. All drank water from the same bucket and tin dipper, or gourd. We never thought of germs.

There was a farm lantern that had a "hang nail" on the corner of the barn for its "residency." Only Dad Lee used the lantern. We Lee boys would go into the stable and feel around to find the end of the mule that was to be bridled. In the cow barn, we would feel around to find which end of the cow to milk!

I milked a cow named Nancy for years at about 4 A.M. each morning, winter and summer. The Massey boys, near neighbors, claimed I did not know what color the cow was for two years.

On the farm, we learned many things in the realm of

Nature

We knew the names of all the trees, vines, shrubs, and weeds. We knew all sorts of snakes—rattlers, black, moccasins, green, and king snakes. We knew about animals. We knew about minks—the marauders by night of the chicken house. We knew about rabbits, 'possums, raccoons, foxes, squirrels, weasels, skunks. We knew about braying mules, neighing horses, mooing cows, bellowing bulls, squealing pigs, grunting hogs, barking dogs and squirrels, cackling hens and crowing roosters, squeaking rats, and the flocks of wild geese honking in their flights to Southern sections and lakes.

We set traps for rats and mice—pestiferous invaders of the corncrib. With a screenless house, we were bothered by filthy flies that made swimming pools out of Mother's bowls of gravy.

Tormented, too, we were by mosquitoes which, with trenchant beaks, sought to fill themselves with blood. In the cow pasture, we sometimes watched tumble bugs, deft dealers in dung, at work.

We often listened, at work and at play, to the songs of the mocking birds—"the Beethovens of the boughs"—and to the piping of the meadow larks, the Mendelssohns of the meadows—along with the squawking chatter of jay birds and the raucous call of the crows.

We learned what some educated folks did not and do not know—the genital period of animals and birds. Small birds require two weeks to hatch. Large ones require three, four, and even six weeks. The genital period of all oval life is a period of a multiple of seven.

Small animals require fewer weeks. Canines require nine weeks, swine twenty weeks, bovines thirty-six weeks, a horse forty-four. We did not know that an elephant requires eighty weeks to generate her young.

Think now, as to the Lee family, of

Clothes

The Lee family had weekday clothes and Sunday clothes, jean breeches, hickory shirts, brogan shoes. I went barefooted much of the time, even to church service. And the soles of my feet became tough, something like leather.

Such makes me think of an old couple in Arkansas who went

barefooted all summer and part of the autumn time. One cold winter night, the old lady was standing with her back to the fire which was burning in the huge fire place. The old man was rocking slowly back and forth in a rocking chair. He took the corncob pipe from between his lips, and said: "Maw!"

"Yes, paw!"

"You're standing on a coal of fire."

"Bees I?"

"Yep!"

"Which foot?"

I think of the

Lee Family Foods

The Lees sometimes had more than enough—and sometimes less than enough. Flour bread was often a scarcity. We had biscuits once a week, usually on Sunday morning for breakfast. In those days when cotton was five cents a pound and flour ten dollars a barrel, when I got a biscuit, the first bite was a half-moon and the second bite a total eclipse!

Later I learned that King Solomon could be called wise because he had twice as much corn bread as he had flour bread. "And Solomon's provision for one day was thirty measures of fine flour, and threescore measures of meal" (1 Kings 4:22).

In hog-killing time there was meat a-plenty—hams, slabs of bacon, chitterlings, and, later, sausage and "cracklins." At hog-killing time, hog bladders were cleaned up, blown up, tied up with strong strings and kept for explosive purposes in noisemaking on Christmas Day.

For food there were peanuts, scuppernongs, watermelons, cantaloupes, cucumbers, cabbages.

On this infertile farm production was poor—no matter how diligent was the cultivation, no matter how much fertilizer, often called guano, was used.

It was with the Lees somewhat as it was with old Steve Potts, a black man who worked hard on a poor farm he rented from a Mr. Sutton. To Sutton, who sold fertilizer, Steve Potts went and said: "Boss man, Steve wants to buy a ton of guano on credit."

"Steve," said Sutton, "Why do you want to buy a ton of guano?"
"To make cotton, suh", said Steve.
"Why do you want to make cotton?" he asked.
"To pay for guano," said Steve soberly.
And thus it was in those days with many renters.

On the farm, drought was a dreadful thing. A horror was a hailstorm, beating the growing crops to the ground. And too much rain, preventing cultivation of the crops, was a menacing matter.

I would have you think now of

Reading in the Lee Family

Few books we had. I remember that *The Youth's Companion* and *The Baptist Courier* and *The Atlanta Constitution* were weekly visitors to the family—after RFD became a reality. In the *Atlanta Constitution* were DeWitt Talmage's sermons published in full. These sermons Dad Lee read to us, sometimes on Sunday afternoon and on winter nights. Those sermons left a great impression on my mind and heart.

These books I remember: *Buffalo Bill, Stepping Heavenward* by Elizabeth Prentiss, some books by G. A. Henty, *Wide, Wide World* by Elizabeth Warner, and *The Sky Pilot* by Ralph Conner. *The Sky Pilot* is the book which influenced my life more than any book except the Bible.

Never did anybody doubt that Noah had an ark—as say some infidel teachers and writers. Today, many are taught to believe that the "flood was probably a disastrous flood in Babylon"; that Methuselah's long life was incompatible with the physical structure; that "Melchizedek was not a priest of God"; that "Moses on Mt. Sinai was only a dramatic picture founded on a thunderstorm"; that "Adam just dreamed about the rib being taken from his side"; that "the tree of knowledge of good and evil was some sort of poison ivy"; that "the story of the fall is a parable based on ancient literary symbolism"; that "the manna was a white secretion from the tamarisk tree"; that "the death of Uzziah was caused by a heart attack or maybe the cart turned over and crushed him"; that "Adam and Eve were driven from the garden by a terrific thunder storm"; that "Daniel never was in the lions' den"; that "Mary mistook the angel Gabriel for a passing stranger";

that "Bible writers had unbalanced minds and rabid imaginations"; that "Jesus did not walk on the water but walked on the shore and the disciples *thought* he was walking on the water"; that "Jesus fainted on the cross and when he was taken down was not dead but in a swoon and the coolness of the grave revived him—and he escaped and appeared to his disciples but died later."

With sober emphasis, my mother said: "Always believe the Bible—all of it—no matter who doesn't believe it."

Today, I write and speak about the Bible these words: "The Bible travels more highways, walks more bypaths, knocks at more doors, and speaks to more people in their mother tongue than any book the world has ever known, can ever know, will ever know."

But it is really my mother speaking through me when I say that the Bible is immeasurable in influence, inexhaustible in adequacy, infallible in authority, personal in application, regenerative in power, inspired in totality, the miracle Book of diversity in unity and of harmony in infinite complexity. And all of its enemies have not torn one hole in its holy vesture nor diluted one drop of the honey of its hive, nor shortened its march of triumph by one step, nor weakened its life by one pulse beat.

So fond was I of reading that I read over and over again some of the few books we had. But of all the books that found lodging in the Lee farmhouse, the Bible was the chief. It was looked upon by all the Lees as the Israelites looked upon the holy of holies or the ark of the covenant.

We believed that monstrously wicked was anybody and everybody who doubted any portion or put a question mark after the miracles. No poison of modernism ever entered the minds and hearts of any of the Lees. Never did the poison ivy of liberal teaching or disbelief enter the Lee home when it came to believing the Bible.

When I consider the intellects of those who disparage and deny Bible truth, I think of the answer given by a listener to a public speaker. The lecturer was a Jewish gentleman who was speaking of the value of vegetarianism and pounding with merciless verbal barrage eaters of meat.

He said: "Every time you eat a piece of ham, it takes one year from your life. Every time you eat a piece of sausage, it takes two years from your life. Every time you eat a piece of bologna, it takes three years from your life."

His eloquent castigation of meat eaters was interruped by a big fat man who got up and started out, running over a chair and creating quite a disturbance.

"Where are you going, friend?" loudly asked the lecturer.

"I am going to the cemetery, sir. According to what you just said, I've been dead two hundred and eighty years!"

So dead think and say I of the intellects of those who use their critical and skeptical knives to cut to pieces the Bible—Book above and beyond all books as a river is beyond a rill in reach.

I think, as to the Lee family, of

Physical Ailments and Medicines

With her children, Mother Lee had to deal with chicken pox, measles, mumps, itch, earache, toothache, colic, and flesh made raw with poison ivy, grippe, whooping cough, and various bruises.

What were the medicines she had? There was Sloan's Liniment—"good for man and beast." Castor oil—the dreadest of all dread purgatives. Mrs. Winslow's Soothing Syrup. Copperas water—used to combat the ravages of poison ivy. Turpentine was used for cuts and bruises. Mustard plasters were used for lung and stomach ailments. The remedy for toothache was usually extraction. Bags of hot ashes were applied for earache. Both patient nurse and faithful physician was Mother Lee.

Now think of the

Work in the Lee Family

Work, hard work, harder than the slaved of ante-bellum days knew, was our lot by day and often by night.

There was no such thing as a five-day week or an eight-hour day. No such thing as starting to work after sunrise or quitting before sunset. Work was the Lee food and the Lee drink. Dad Lee, a rigid disciplinarian, and a hard worker himself, demanded such of all his sons and all the few hired servants.

Many times the mule I plowed was hitched to the plow before it was light enough to see the furrow. Many times I plowed until the darkness came after the sunset.

Dad Lee sometimes would call out in early morning to the children: "Get up Jim! Get up, Fanny! Get up, Ben! Get up, Frank! Get up, Bob! Get up, Tom! Today is Monday. Next day is Tuesday, next day is Wednesday! Half the week gone and nothing done!"

Pulling fodder, when the puller looked into the sun as he reached for the top leaves on the corn stalk and bent down with the sun beaming on his back, was an ordeal. Picking cotton when the sun made the field a furnace or when the frost chilled the fingers on autumn mornings, was strenuous work. But, despite the heat, despite the frost at times, some days I picked over three hundred pounds. Cutting wheat with a wheat cradle made many muscles sore and the back burdensomely tired. Plowing cotton and corn in the hot weather left the clothes often soaked with sweat—not a dry thread in the shirt, not a dry spot on the trousers.

Sometimes when rains came and no work could be done in the field, my Dad would say: "Now while we are resting, let's shuck some corn or cut some stove wood." Many hours have I spent on rainy days, shucking corn or chopping wood in the woodshed—"while we rested."

Many times I carried a one-hundred pound sack of fertilizer across an acre of plowed ground. Many times, I used the axe in cutting down trees and splitting rails to build the rail fence pasture.

Many times with the hoe I "chopped cotton" until my hands were blistered and later became calloused. Many times I welcomed the short days and long nights of winter even though "late to bed and early to rise" was often the rule of the Lee household. I have done everything on the farm from greasing a gimlet to riding a bucking mule.

In the nighttime, we heard the weird wailing of the whippoorwills, the mournful dirges of the hoot owls, and the wild cries of the screech owls. We heard often the crowing of roosters before dawn. Working in the fields, we sometimes took note of buzzards circling in the sky with eyes keen for carrion.

On the farm we found necessary and most useful two gray mules—Ben and Barney. They knew the meaning of "gee!" and "haw!" When we said "gee," they turned to the right. When we said "haw," they turned to the left. Of much joy were the two shepherd dogs—Zack and Zeb. If I could have gotten some church members to be as obedient in work as were Ben and Barney and as faithful as were Zack and Zeb, greater work would the churches have done.

Rest periods on the farm—with the exception of Sundays and when we were in bed—were as scarce as showers in the Sahara Desert.

But now, looking back after all these years, I am glad that such was so. Why? Because it prepared me for the early hours of getting up, the many long hours of work I have done—both mental and physical—in my pastorates.

2

Early Churches in My Life

My Boyhood Church

First, I make mention of my boyhood church in Fort Mill, South Carolina, the First Baptist Church where my mother was a charter member. As a young woman, she used to walk barefooted six miles to this little house of God—carrying her button shoes and stockings in her hand. At the outdoor pool, she would, before church services began, wash her feet, put on her stockings and shoes, and go in to worship in the little house of God.

In this boyhood church, I went to Sunday School, to the Sunbeam Band, made my public confession of faith in Jesus, was baptized August 5, 1898, and, two years later, I taught a Sunday School class of boys just a bit younger than I.

My sister, Fanny, played the organ—a "pump" organ—in this church.

In this church house, April 3, 1910, I was ordained to the gospel ministry, after a public examination as to my belief as to certain doctrines and after a statement as to my Christian experience in being saved. Looking back, I remember that as a freshman in Furman University, I had to borrow money from one of my professors to buy my train ticket to Fort Mill and back to Greenville, South Carolina.

All hands placed on my head that night, including my father's work-hardened hands, have long been still in the dust of the grave. But I thank God for all of them.

August 5, 1973, the folks of my boyhood church had me back to preach as they observed the seventy-fifth anniversary of my baptism on August 5, 1898. The pastor and church presented me with a color picture beautifully framed of the outdoor pool where my parents were baptized over one hundred years ago. The pool fed by a clear-water spring is still there, though never used in baptisms anymore.

Lima Baptist Church

I think that with most folks first things are of interest. With some, it is the first date with the opposite sex. With some, it is the first money earned. With some, winning the first athletic contest. With some fellows, it is the first kiss some lovely girl with luscious lips gives.

But of more interest to me was my first pastorate—more interesting than my first suit of clothes or my first date with a girl or my first sermon or the first kiss I got from the sweet lady whom I married.

My first little church—LIMA—in the North Greenville Association, called me on recommendation of my Bible teacher and president of Furman University, Dr. E. M. Poteat. This little church had fifty-three members. My salary was fifty dollars a year for one visit a month. I preached Saturday afternoon and Sunday morning and went back to my college dorm.

After I had been pastor at Lima for one year, an effort on the part of a few benevolent-minded members was made to raise my salary to seventy-five dollars a year for one visit a month with preaching Saturday afternoon and Sunday morning—the fourth Sunday in each month. With perfect parliamentary procedure, the motion was made and duly seconded in a cnurch conference. Remarks were called for by the chairman of the ueacons who presided as moderator. Brother Burrell Cox, a kindly man, with the attitude of a "ruler of the synagogue," arose from his seat near one of the windows, and said: "Brethren and sisters, I love our young preacher as much as any of you'uns, but we-uns can't afford to bite off more than we can chew or swallow or digest, an' as fur as I'm concerned, we're already payin' fur as much as we're gittin.'" To this I agreed, and I was not disappointed when the church voted not to raise my salary.

At this little church, one fifth Sunday in November, I baptized nineteen young people in a cold, outdoor pool at which time a thin skin of ice was raked off. That was as cold as I have ever been—even colder than when in Duluth, Minnesota, the thermometer went to thirty degrees below zero during the days of my preaching there.

At this little Lima Church, a sweet little widow, mother of twelve children, came to my rescue on one occasion. I was carrying newspapers at that time in Greenville, South Carolina, getting up at 3:00 A.M. each day to distribute the newspaper to designated places.

One day on my way to the Latin class, I stopped by the campus post office. There I received a notice from Dean Cox. He wrote: "Mister Lee: I know you have some financial difficulties, but you owe the University $84.00. The auditors will be examining the books this coming Monday, and I hope you will see to it that the eighty-four dollars is paid before then."

In the Latin class, it looked as though Professor Matin had an eighty-four on his nose glasses. When I went back to my room #3 in Griffith Cottage, it seemed as though the #3 above the door had twisted itself into an eighty-four. Inside the room, the alarm clock that awoke me at 3:00 A.M. seemed to be clicking out the words, "84,84,84." I pulled down the shade. I got down on my knees and talked to God. And I did not pray any "Polly-wants-a-cracker" prayer. I talked to God about his saving me and calling me to preach. And I said: "I don't know anybody in the world to whom I can go and get eighty-four bucks. Help me, Lord, Help me!"

On Saturday morning, I went up to the mountains on the little train which was called the "Swamp Rabbit Special." I was met at the swampy small station and taken to the church. I preached that afternoon. At the close of the service, the twenty-seven people who were there sang "Rescue the Perishing." I needed rescue. But from whom?

That night, I went to the home of a little widow. With her and some of her children and grandchildren, I ate supper. About ten o'clock, I said: "I need to go to bed. Let us have some prayer."

I quoted some verses from Psalm 34 and prayed. I started up the stairs to "the prophet's room." When I got to the halfway landing of the stairway, the little widow said: "Mister Lee, wait a minute. I don't know why I have not thought of it before. But yesterday, I got to thinking of how you are working your way through college and you might need a little help."

I said, "Yes, ma'am."

In a downstairs room behind the bulge of the stairway, I heard the unlocking and slamming of some sort of trunk lid. She came up the steps and said to me: "Now shut your eyes and hold out your hands."

I shut these eyes, though they did not have glasses on them. I held out these two hands, except they were lots stronger than they are now. Then she dropped something into my outstretched hands.

"Now, open your eyes," she said. I looked and saw five-dollar gold pieces in my hands—twenty of them! The Aurora Borealis, a gorgeous sunrise, a golden sunset, all combined, could not have been more beautiful to see.

I began to laugh and cry. And it is none of your business what else I did. I took the twenty five-dollar gold pieces, not asking how she got them or how long she had kept them hidden away in some old trunk.

I put the five-dollar gold pieces on twenty squares of the quilt on the old four-poster bed, and, on my knees with grateful heart, I viewed that golden landscape o'er, thanking God for his goodness to me through a little widow.

From that hour, I called this little widow my second mother. And her picture is framed now in my bedroom between the picture of my own mother and my wife's mother.

Sweet and grateful are all the memories I have and hold of the kind helpfulness and helpful kindness of the folks at Lima and the folks of some other mountain churches where I had the honor and joy to preach on occasions.

The pulpit stand, a huge wooden "affair" put together with wood nails, is in the chapel at the Bellevue Baptist Church,. And the pulpit chair, which is not a chair but a wooden bench eight feet long with a wood back is in the Lee Momento House in the Lee Memorial Garden across Court Street from the Bellevue Church house of God. Both are about one hundred and fifty years old. I never see them but what acknowledgement of God's goodness to me floods my heart.

Two men named Cox went out from this little church to become late millionaires. Elzie Cox—in Seattle, Washington—became a millionaire. All the land that the World's Fair in Seattle used was bought from Elzie. And the Needle, with the dining room on top, was built on the spot where Elzie had his real estate office.

Some weeks before he died, Elzie left $25,000 to three churches—Lima, Cox's Chapel, and another mountain church, for the upkeep for years of the cemeteries at these churches.

And Fred Cox, son of Arthur Cox, deacon of the Lima Baptist Church, went to Oklahoma. And, living near Tulsa, he became a millionaire.

An unusually unique truth from such a small mountain church.

Fairview Baptist Church

There was the *Fairview* Baptist Church in Greenville County—the second church to extend me a call.

At the first business conference at Fairview, an argument arose between two of the brethren. It was ultimately settled with fists outside the church. The cause of the argument was known only to the participants.

Very vividly was the blood brought to one member's face by the fist of the other. Very vividly, too, in my memory is the Sunday morning scene when the two brethren who had fought until they were bruised and bloody, arose together in church, asking the church to forgive them for their unchristian conduct, and receiving such a formal vote of the membership, shook hands and sat down together in the same pew and sang out of the same hymnbook.

There on March 3, 1910, I held my first funeral service—one month before I became an ordained minister.

Putting this little girl, Katie Lanford, in the ground was not like some funerals I saw when I was a boy, when the coffin was let down six feet into the ground. Then neighbors would shovel in the dirt on the coffin of the dead. I recall how horribly terrible was the sound of clods and dirt upon the coffin lid. And after the grave was filled and a mound of earth made, flowers were placed on the dirt mound before people turned sorrowfully and sympathetically away.

At Fairview Baptist Church, I was pastor of the dear old highly honored and devotedly loved pioneer preacher, Ben Vaughan. Memories of him and his dedicated life and his encouragement to me as a young preacher are like fragrant and lovely flowers in the garden of my life.

I preached in a revival meeting at the church after Dr. E. S. Reeves, who baptized me and whom I had invited to preach during the days of revival effort, became so hoarse he could not preach. God blessed and many were saved. There I later baptized in an outdoor pool.

Harmony Baptist Church

The Harmony Baptist Church in Laurens County, South Carolina, was the third church to extend a call to me. This church, too, as was the case with all the churches which ever called me, called me without having seen or having heard me.

The salary at the church was one hundred dollars a year, paid every two months.

At Harmony I actually did my first baptizing. The one baptized was little Bertha Lee Helms, a twelve-year-old girl. At twenty, she married and later became the mother of four sons. All of these sons were reared and nurtured in the ways of the Lord by their parents and became deacons in a Baptist church.

When Bertha died, one of the sons 'phoned me saying the mother's request was before she died, that I should conduct her funeral services. I flew from Memphis and held the service, after visiting the night before among the neighbors who gathered at her house to "look upon her face" and to speak words of sympathy to the bereaved loved ones.

At Harmony, I presided for the first time in the observance by the church of the Lord's Supper.

At Harmony, I received the first money I ever received for preaching—$16.80 given me by W. S. Power, treasurer of the church. I have a framed photograph of his hands—the hands that gave me my first money as pastor. Later, when I visited this good man in a convalescent home, I mentioned the fact to him, both as to the $16.80 he gave and the framed photograph of his hands. Soberly, this good man with serious quietness said: "I was embarrassed over the $16.80, and the Harmony Church should blush a long time over their guilt in not doing more for a young preacher working his way through college."

At Harmony, the crude dressing house for those who are to be baptized is still there—much weather worn—after all these years. Moreover, the heavy picnic tables made of thick slabs of lumber are still on the church grounds—ready for the Sundays of "dinner on the grounds." In many houses of members of Harmony, I was the beneficiary of gracious hospitality, manifested particularly in the abundance of all sorts of food placed on the dining room tables.

After I had preached one Saturday afternoon in September, 1910, at the Lima Baptist Church, where I had been pastor for five months, Will Goodwin told me that at the New Liberty Baptist Church they were having a "protracted meeting" and that the pastor was doing the preaching. I had never heard the Reverend Mullinnix, the pastor, a mountain preacher of good report. So I asked Will Goodwin, at whose home I was to spend the night, to take me that night to the meeting.

Though the church was seven miles from Will's house, he said he had a buggy and a good horse and he would drive me there. It took us longer to go the seven miles than we thought. And we got to the New Liberty Baptist Church about fifteen minutes late. I took a look at the cemetery, after Will had hitched his horse to a post. The full moon was shining on the tombstones that glowed with snow-white brightness in the moonlight. I looked at the many horses and buggies and wagons on the hitching ground. And the church was "cram-jam" with folks—all pews occupied, an overflow choir loft, and some people standing.

Will and I took our places with others standing near the door. After the choir and congregation had sung two or three gospel hymns, the pastor, this mountain preacher who had a county-wide reputation for eloquence and sound doctrine in his preaching, looked my way.

He said: "Brethren and sisters and friends, I see our young brother, Robert Lee, pastor of Lima, standing back there. He will preach for us in a short while."

I was stunned. With a sort of stutter, I said: "Brother Mullinnix,

I don't have any sermon, and I am not ready. I don't have but about ten sermons to my name."

"Oh, young brother, the Lord will give you something to say to us."

I turned to Will and said: "What shall I do?"

Will answered: "What he says." Then Brother Mullinnix said: "Will our young brother come forward and occupy this chair on the pulpit platform?"

I gave my hat to Will. Embarrassedly shocked, I walked down the aisle. As I walked I prayed: "O, Lord, give me something to say."

Brother Mullinnix struck out his big hand and pointed me to a chair on the platform. I sat down, confusedly embarrassed and in mental distress.

Then the thought of the astronomy examination I had gone through the previous week at Furman University came to me. And then, Psalm 84:11 came to my mind: "For the Lord God is a sun and shield: the Lord will give grace and glory: no good thing will he withhold from them that walk uprightly" (Ps. 84:11).

I took this verse as my text. I said: "Since God is a sun, He will give us light in darkness—the darkness of life. Since God is a shield, He will be protection to us in the battle of life." Then I gave the congregation what I had put on my astronomy examination.

I told the folks that when I was a boy on the farm, my mother used to make what we called a cherry pan pie. She would take a big dish pan, fill it with cherries and cherry juice, pour in sugar, put on and in the proper crust and tell her boys to come and eat. That summons the Lee boys gladly and greedily obeyed, sometimes gorging ourselves.

Then I said that we should suppose we had a pan as big as the sun and fill it with cherries—each cherry as big as the earth—25,000 miles around the earth and 8,000 miles through the earth and we should make a pan pie out of the materials assembled.

Then following this supposition, I asked: "Do you know how many cherries, each cherry as big as the earth, it would take to fill the pan if the pan were as big as the sun?"

It would take one million, four hundred thousand cherries, each cherry as big as this earth, and it would take several thousand train-loads of sugar to sweeten it and all the surveyors in the United States quite a time to measure the crust.

The earth goes around the sun on its annual journey five hundred and fifty-eight million miles at a speed of sixty-eight thousand miles an hour. It is warmed by the sun, which is nearly one hundred thousand million miles away, and is surrounded by an ocean of ether at absolute zero, through which it whirls on its axis at the rate of nineteen miles per second.

Mars, two hundred million miles away, goes around the sun once in six hundred and twenty-seven days at a speed of forty-nine thousand miles an hour in its orbit.

Saturn, eight hundred and eighty-five million miles away, goes around the sun once in thirty years at a speed of twenty-one thousand miles per hour. Going at a rate of one hundred and fifty miles per hour, it would take us 1,470 years to reach that planet.

Uranus, one billion, seven hundred and eighty million miles away, goes around the sun once in eighty years at a speed of two hundred and fifty miles an hour. Traveling at a rate of sixty miles an hour, it would take us three thousand, one hundred and sixty years to reach old Uranus. And Uranus has six moons. These satellites of Uranus advance from east to west. All satellites of all other planets advance from west to east.

So go the earth around the sun and Mars in its journey, and Uranus. But not the satellites of Uranus. They advance from east to west in retrograde motion, in reverse gear, all the time.

I told the folks that all such wonders prove that there is an all-wise, all-powerful God who operates the universe and that this one who inhabits eternity also dwells with people who are of humble and contrite hearts.

I said: "This year there has been much mention in the newspaper and in private conversations of Halley's comet. On May 5, 1910, the length of the tail of Halley's comet was thirty-seven million miles. On May 20, 1910, this comet was its least distance from the earth—

fourteen million miles. The speed of this comet varies from one to thirty-four miles a second. In 1985 this comet will return, not one minute ahead nor one minute behind its God-appointed schedule. Yet, in the amazing movements of the heavenly bodies, there is no collision.

Then, as I closed my "astronomy" sermon, I said that the great God who guides the planets in their orbits at different speeds could and would guide each life yielded to him—would guide that life from bondage to liberty, from darkness to light, from wickedness to righteousness, from death to life, from damnation to salvation. And I quoted the last part of the text with strong emphasis: "No good thing will he withhold from them who walk uprightly." And I urged them to believe that nobody ever walks uprightly without Jesus as Savior and guide.

And I said that the great God who numbers all the stars in the Milky Way numbers the hairs of our heads. I said: "The creative hand that threw the stars into space is the hand that will hold your hand in the dangerous situations of life and when the shadows of death come.

To add meaning to my own words, I quoted some verses I had memorized when in my teens:

Thus saith God the Lord, he that created the heavens, and stretched them out; he that spread forth the earth, and that which cometh out of it; he that giveth breath unto the people upon it, and spirit to them that walk therein. I the Lord have called thee in righteousness (Isa. 42:5-6).

I, even I, am he that blotteth out thy transgressions for mine own sake, and will not remember thy sins (Isa. 43:25).

Fear thou not; for I am with thee: be not dismayed; for I am thy God: I will help thee; yea, I will uphold thee with the right hand of my righteousness (Isa. 41:10).

When I had finished and had taken my seat, the tall, kind-faced and gracious pastor, turned to me and said, in a quiet voice: "Call the mourners! Call the mourners!"

I think I was the biggest mourner in the house. But I asked them to sing a hymn after I had "invited the mourners." Several people, men and women, came forward, with tears, "confessing their sins" and asking prayers of God's people.

May my tongue cleave to the roof of my mouth if ever I think of or speak of that night without gratitude in my heart.

3.
First Baptist Church, Edgefield, South Carolina

After serving as pastor of some country churches—Fairview, Harmony, Coneross, Durbin, and Beulah—and of four little town churches—Waterloo, Mountville, Cross Hill, and Princeton—I became pastor of the Red Bank Baptist Church in Saluda—the countyseat of Saluda County.

There began an event in my life that borders on the nightmaric in some respects. For years I had held the ambition, almost an obsession, to be a college professor and a pastor at the same time. It seemed at first as though the realization of my ambition was having a sunrise.

Why? The president of Furman University, my alma mater, and the Board of Trustees elected me to be head of the Latin-Spanish department at Furman. I was not to be an assistant or tutor but head of the Latin Department made vacant by the resignation of Professor C. B. Martin who had been my Latin teacher. Dr. Poteat assured me that I could hold a pastorate and a professorship at "one and the same time."

I resigned at Red Bank where I was serving when World War I startled the nations. I resigned my Red Bank pastorate, and at the suggestion of Dr. E. M. Poteat, president of Furman, I decided to go to Tulane University for some intensive study in Latin and Spanish.

Two days before I was to depart for New Orleans and Tulane University, the pulpit committee from the First Baptist Church, Union, South Carolina, visited me and offered me the pastorate of First Baptist Church in Union, South Carolina—offering a salary that seemed fabulous. They begged me ("with no reflection on my decision) not to go to Tulane but to accept their offer and come to Union, First Baptist Church. While I appreciated their offer and their plea, I was adamantly determined to go to Tulane. I did. Leaving my wife and little daughter in Greenville in a "ramshackle little shack" of a home, I went to Tulane. For three months I studied diligently much by day and much by night, paying board and living a *lonesome* life away from my wife and child.

In September of that year—having had no income and paying rent on a shack of a little home hardly fit to live in—I returned to Greenville with the purpose to be pastor of some church as well as professor of the Latin-Spanish Department.

After talking together and after prayer, my wife and I decided to build a little home, if I could borrow the money necessary to build. I went to Mr. McGee, president of a National Bank, and asked if I could borrow enough money to build a little bungalow near the Furman campus.

This good man said: "Mr. Lee, I'll let you have the money, but I think I should tell you something before you go further. I am a trustee of Furman. At our last trustee meeting, the trustees voted that none of the new professors could hold a pastorate and head a department in Furman."

Startled, I said: "But Dr. Poteat promised me I could so do."

"But Dr. Poteat has resigned, and the trustees voted as I have said."

Shocked, I went to work and called for a meeting of all the trustees that could meet on a certain date, asking Dr. Poteat to be present. They met in a business office in Greenville, the president being there. I met with them and asked if their vote a week or so ago meant that I should not hold a pastorate along with my teaching duties.

The chairman of the board said, very courteously, with a tinge of pity in his words: "Yes, Mr. Lee, you know a pastorate is a big job and a professorship is a big job and, while you are a brilliant-minded young man. I doubt if you are big enough to hold both jobs effectively."

I said: "Well, gentlemen, without any bitterness in my heart and without any criticism of you, I offer my resignation. I would not give up my preaching to be president of the United States."

They accepted my resignation, and a vote was made that I be paid the expenses I incurred for my three months at Tulane. I guess that vote was forgotten or overlooked because my expenses were never paid. And I did not ask that they be paid.

After the close of the meeting, President Poteat and I walked together down the street—both of us silent for a block. Then Dr. Poteat said: "I am sorry, Mr. Lee. Those fellows don't know your ability. What do you plan to do now?"

"God will guide me," was all I said.

I walked a mile to the little shack of an apartment for which I had paid rent and where the three Lees were staying. There was one door to that little shack. And the lady to whom I paid rent was mean. She could forget her birthday or Thanksgiving or Christmas more easily than she could forget the day the rent was due.

There was just one door—a back door—to the shack apartment. My wife was standing in the doorway with my little two-year-old girl in her arms. I said to her: "Well, honey, you have a husband without a job."

"Why?" she asked in amazement.

I said: "I resigned my place as head of the Latin-Spanish Department at Furman because they said I could not hold a pastorate."

"That's good," said my wife. "God never meant for you to be digging around among Latin roots and Spanish stumps. God meant for you to be a preacher."

There were only a few dollars and a scanty supper, but much prayer in that little shack that night. And much prayer in the dreary days that followed. I managed to borrow some money, without any endorsement on my note, from Mr. McGee. We used the money to "live on"—rent, groceries, necessary clothes.

I asked nobody for a job. I asked nobody to recommend me to some church. We just prayed.

In November—two months after I resigned at Furman—the First Baptist Church of Edgefield "in conference assembled," extended me a call. They had never seen me. I had never seen them. They asked me to visit and "occupy the pulpit" and "see how I liked them."

I wired them I would not do that—and that I did not want anyone to think I was preaching "a trial sermon." But I accepted their call.

Packing up what little furniture and other things we had, the three Lees, happy as could be, took the train to Augusta and from Augusta to Edgefield.

When we arrived at the railroad station in Edgefield, there were nineteen coffins on the platform—because the terrible flu epidemic was on, and strong men were going to their deaths like rills rushing to a river.

The chairman of the pulpit committee met us, greeted us happily, then sorrowfully mentioned the nineteen coffins.

We found a little three-room house with a kitchen attached. There was a hole in the kitchen roof. I had to hold an umbrella over the skillet while my wife cooked or fried eggs or bacon if it were raining. In two weeks I had the hole fixed.

The little house was close by the roadside, and clouds of dust, when the weather was dry, covered the porch and front of the house. My salary was $1800 a year, with "the preacher to furnish his own home."

The flu epidemic would not permit church services for four weeks. The E. J. Norris family took the three Lees into their home while we waited for the household stuff to arrive by freight.

I took the flu and nearly died. Some did while I was sick.

At last church services were permitted, and the dear folks came to "see if that young fellow Lee knew anything about preaching." Well! I was glad that God, in a strangely mysterious way, took away my ambition and killed my obsession to be a pastor-professor "all in one."

Blessedly happy the days of our pastorate there, even though I had to borrow some money "to meet expenses." One morning, at the breakfast table, I said to my little wife, "Do you know what's on today?"

"Yes," she said, "you have a note due for one hundred dollars—and you can't pay it."

"What shall I do?"

"Ask Mr. Mims to renew it."

"But I have done that once, and I don't want to do it again. I may get the reputation of being careless or neglectful about money matters."

"But there is nothing else you can do," she said.

"Let us pray about it."

After breakfast, I screwed up my courage to the sticking place and was on my way to the bank to ask for a renewal of my note. As I started across the town square to the bank, a big chunky man, a Mr. Hollingsworth, called me across the street and said: "I sold my cotton this morning. Got a good price for it. And I thought my pastor might need a little money."

"Yes," I said, "you're right."

He pulled out of one of the big pockets of his overalls, a big roll of money bills. There was the five dollar layer, and the ten dollar layer and the twenty dollar layer, and the fifty dollar layer. Then he came to the hundred dollar section of the roll of bills. Talk about geological strata! No such could have so much interest for me.

He handed me a hundred dollar bill. I burst into tears. He said: "Don't make a fool out of yourself."

"I'll be as big a fool as I please!" I said.

I took that hundred dollar bill and started home. When I got half way across the public square he shouted: "Come back here!" Well, I put the brake on my two-cylinders and stopped. I did not want to go back. I thought maybe he had made a mistake and had given me one hundred when he meant to give me ten.

With a bit of reluctance, I went back to him. He took me in a butcher shop and bought me a whole quarter of beef. He put the quarter of "old Sooky" on my shoulder and said, "Now go home and eat till you bust."

With that quarter of a cow on my shoulder and that one hundred dollars in my hand, I went back to our little home. My wife met me at the door.

"What is that you have?" she asked.

"A quarter of a cow and a fence post with two goose eggs beside," I said, with a glad laugh. I showed her the hundred dollar bill. "Where did you get that?" she asked. I told her.

Blessed day that! The note paid. And much beef to eat.

At Edgefield, another strange thing was done. I was pastor at the Horn's Creek church, where I preached on Sunday afternoon. The church had gone out of business. It was reactivated. One night during the hour of reactivation, the people voted for me to take a drink of water.

Here is how it came about. Dr. W. G. Johnson first president of the Southern Baptist Convention, had been pastor at the First Baptist Church of Edgefield and at Horn's Creek, too. The cup out of which he had drunk water was on the pulpit stand, full of water. The people wanted me to drink out of it as one who was pastor when Dr. Johnson had been pastor. I refused, saying: "No. I do not think I am worthy to drink out of the cup." But a motion was made and seconded and a vote was taken that I drink "out of Dr. Johnson's cup." I did, feeling that my lips were touching holy silver. I do not know of any other church voting for their pastor to take a drink of water.

But the most wonderful of all Edgefield events during my days in the town was when the people paid off the church debt. That debt of $11,000 on which 8 percent was being paid, bothered and burdened me. To me that debt, with recurring 8 percent interest payments was a painful "thorn in the flesh."

One night, down on my knees in a little niche in the house I called my study, I sought direction from God. A voice—the voice of God, I believe—spoke with an authoritative whisper, saying: "Quit praying. I have heard your prayer. Go to bed and sleep. Then next Sunday ask the people to pay the debt off, and they will."

At breakfast the next morning, I said to Lady Lee, "Do you know what I am going to do?" Incidentally, she said: "No telling!" (She said that all the fifty-seven years we lived together: "No telling what my husband will say if he believes he should say it. No telling what he will do if he believes he ought to do it.")

I said: "Next Sunday, I am going to announce that on the following Sunday the people are going to pay off the church debt. And I am not going to say a word to any deacon; not a word to anyone but you, and you must not tell it."

Lady Lee said: "I am not going to tell it, but do you know what you are doing?"

"Yes. I got it from God."

Next Sunday morning, as we walked our way to the house of God, my wife, with some doubt as to the wisdom of my proposed announcement, quietly asked "Do you still believe you should make the announcement about paying the church debt next Sunday?"

"Yes. I am going to make the announcement, though I have told nobody."

The church met for worship. Nearly all the members were present including former Governor John Shepard with his silver-headed walking stick.

After we had sung an hymn, I said: "Brethren and sisters, I am going to make an announcement. I have not told anybody what I am going to say except my wife and God. Nobody else knows about this announcement. But next Sunday morning, we are going to pay off our church debt."

Governor Shepard, his cane waving back and forth in his agitated hand, sprang to his feet. "Do I hear my ears aright?" he loudly asked.

His brother, Orlando Shepard, clerk of the church, answered the governor. And he emphasized the word *young* more than he did the word "preacher."

I spoke: "Yes, Governor, you heard your ears aright. Next Sunday, we will pay off our church debt. Together we can do it. Together the links make the chain. Together the trees make the forest. Together the shingles make the roof. Together the soldiers make the army. But nobody must give over five hundred dollars. I will give back any amount that goes beyond five hundred dollars. I want *everybody* to give, and all that is given must be cash or a check that will not bounce. Next Sunday is the day."

Had I thrown exploding dynamite on the church lawn, I could hardly have startled the people more.

District Attorney Thurmond made this comment: "Fine young preacher but very impractical."

There was talking among the members as they left the church grounds. All over town that afternoon, there was talking. All through the week, there was much talking—in the stores, the barber shop, in offices, in homes, on street corners, and most of it about the debt-paying.

When I went to town, many would ask me if I thought I would get enough money to pay off the church debt. My answer was: "Yes, unless God dies. You haven't heard of him being dead, have you?"

Wednesday of that week I was walking along Main Street. B. B. Jones, owner of a furniture store, and bank and farm and big dwelling house, called to me from across the street. I went across the street to where he was standing in front of his big store. He reached out his hand to me—this man who had not attended a church service since I became pastor. He said, "You are the new preacher, aren't you?"

"Yes," I answered, "where have you been all the time since I came?"

"I understand," he said, "that you announced that you were going to pay off the church debt next Sunday."

"I announced that *they* were going to pay it off," I said.

"And you told nobody about it before your announcement."

"That's right."

"And I was told that you told the folks that all given must be in cash or good checks."

"That's right."

"And you said you wanted *everybody* to give, but that nobody must give over five hundred dollars."

"That's right, too."

"Well," said this Jones man, "you have less sense or more grit than any preacher that ever came to this town."

He took me back into his office; took out a check book and wrote me out a check for five hundred dollars, with a scratchy old pen. But the scratching of that pen was sweet music to me, sweeter than the chiming of church bells.

He gave me the check and said: "If anybody asks you if Bray Jones is going to give anything just tell 'em what you please." I folded that check and put it in my pocket. I would walk along and take that check out, and thank God.

Three men were standing on the street corner. I passed them by as though I had not seen them.

"Hey, preacher!" one said, "Aren't you going to speak to us?"

I said: "That depends. If you are not going to pay anything on the church debt, you are not worth speaking to."

I walked on.

"Where are you going?" one called after me.

"To the hospital."

"To the hospital? For what?"

"To have my ears moved back, so that my face can hold my smile next Sunday when we pay off the church debt."

Most interesting the times I had that week listening to comments and answering questions about the debt-payment matter.

That Saturday night a big thunderstorm and rain came. "Jupiter Pluvius" seemed to be on a triple drunk. Water—muddy water—everywhere. But, despite the rain, the folks were at church. The church was packed with folks. Not a vacant seat. We sang a hymn and I prayed.

Then I said: "Now, dear folks, the time has come for us to pay off our church debt."

Governor Shepard, his gold-headed walking cane moving back and forth vigorously, arose. "I want to have the honor of giving the first five hundred dollars," he said, loudly.

I said: "I am sorry, Governor, but somebody beat you to it. Bray Jones gave me five hundred dollars the other day." I dropped Bray Jones' check upon the table beneath the pulpit stand.

"Now, Governor," I said, "What I want the folks to do is stand up, tell how much they are giving, and bring it down to this table."

"My name is John C. Shepard. I will give you five hundred dollars." The governor, dressed in a long-tail coat with white vest and striped trousers, waving his gold-headed walking cane, came down the aisle and dropped his check on the table.

Then Abner Broadwater and his little wife stood up. He was the largest man physically I have ever been pastor of. And one of the politest, too. I saw him get up one day and give his seat to *three ladies!*

"My name is Abner Broadwater," he said. "I'll give you five hundred dollars." His wife said: "I'll give you two hundred."

I said, "Mrs. Broadwater, is that your money? You know I said nobody must give over five hundred." She said: "Yes, he has nothing to do with my money."

"Come on down, honey," I said.

Mr. Hollingsworth, the most timid man I ever knew, from a back seat, raised his hand with five fingers spread out. I asked one of the ushers to bring his five hundred down because I knew his timidity would prevent his speaking or coming down the aisle.

Bettis Centalon (whom I called Bettis CanteLOPE) promised two hundred and fifty dollars. Miss Gladys Lyon, who worked in the ten-cent store, arose and said: "My name is Gladys Lyon. I'll give one hundred."

Freckled-face little Billy Hilton stood up: "I'll give five bucks—all I got," he said.

And thus it went until all, young and old, the poor and the rich, had given something.

"Now," I said, "if everybody has given something, I'll ask Brother Lott, our treasurer, to take the money and go into a back room and count it—and I'll send along two deacons to chaperone him."

Brother Lott swept all the money from the table into a good-size basket and went back for the counting. While the money was being counted, the congregation and choir sang some hymns. Back came Brother Lott and the chaperoning deacons. There was a hush over the assembly.

Brother Lott, tears on his cheeks, a tremble in his voice looked at me and said: "Pastor, it has all been counted, and the people have given $14,000."

There were whispers and voices buzzing all over the congregation.

Bray Jones was there, the first time he had been at church since I became pastor. He arose to speak. People became quiet to hear what he said.

"Folks, I want to ask your forgiveness. I have asked God to forgive

me, and he has. This is the first time I have been at church since
Pastor Lee came. And I am ashamed of the little old shack of a
house he is living in down by the roadside. I make a motion that
we add to the money we don't need to pay the debt and build him
a new house and make him chairman of the building committee.
The people voted it. I found myself chairman of a building committee.
I selected Bray Jones, Abner Broadwater, and Bettis Centalon to serve.
And we built a ten-room house. I was hopeful in "them thar days."

The lovely and commodious parsonage of the First Baptist Church,
Edgefield, is there today. And the people call it"The House Lee Built."
I did not. But God's people did, proving that no church ever tests
the resources of God until the membership attempts the impossible,
and when God asks it his people can remove mountains instead of
rolling marbles.

At Edgefield, I asked all members of the board of deacons to resign.
They did, and they gave the newly elected deacons a banquet. It
was at Edgefield, I first delivered and then wrote my "Payday Someday" sermon which I have preached about twelve hundred times in
every state in the United States except two. A moving picture has
been made from this sermon. A sacred opera based on this sermon
has been given. Over eight thousand persons have confessed their
faith in Jesus under the preaching of this sermon.

At Edgefield, in the new parsonage, our little daughter desperately
ill with pneumonia and whooping cough, nearly died. But because
of the service of dear old Dr. Thompson and in answer to prayer,
God spared her. She grew up to be a graduate of Blue Mountain
College and the wife of Rear Admiral E. R. King (retired) of the
United States Navy.

4.
First Baptist Church, Chester, South Carolina

I left the First Baptist Church of Edgefield, and became the pastor of the First Baptist Church, Chester, South Carolina, a lovely little city of ten thousand population. Chester was only thirty five miles from my birthplace.

My brother, Frank, and his wife were members of this church. I had never preached in Chester. By faith the church called me. By faith, I accepted the call. My first sermon was entitled "From Feet to Fathoms," the text being Acts 27:28.

I spoke of the tragedy of churches going from the deep to the shallows in activities. And of the glory of a church going from the shallows to the deeps in service. This first sermon of mine on my first Sunday as pastor prophesied that great achievements would be a reality and not merely a dream or hope—that the church would clothe itself in more vigorous realities and would engage in moving mountains and not rolling marbles.

In this sermon, I urged the church members to believe that we could, under God, flow like rivers and not trickle like rills, shine like chandeliers and not flicker like feeble candles.

This proved to be the case, as proven in that Sunday School and Training Union attendance and the church membership doubled in the sixteen months of my pastorate there. And the treasurer of the church said that more money had come in than ever before, as he understood the financial health of the church.

I determined to visit every home and business office in the membership. I found my visitation work was very profitable to me and to those visited. I found that some houses—some small and cheap, some big and costly in structure—did not have homes in them. I found, too, that some business offices had never had a preacher to pray in them.

Some folks in some homes I visited said: "This is the first time a preacher has been in our home, and we've been here for years." This brings me to say that in this day, pastors who do not visit and learn something of the homelife and business life of their members cheat themselves and rob their members, young and old of the riches they should have.

Looking back to the days of my youth, I remember that great occasion when the pastor visited our farm house and ate at the Lee table. We had more to eat than at other times. Once, a pastor, eating at the table of one family in the membership, said: "I hardly ever have a meal like this."

"We don't either," frankly said the eight-year-old son.

Once I met on the street a man whom I had baptized. The man said to me: "Pastor, I am fifty-two, and in all my life, I ain't never et with a preacher."

I said: "Well, it's lunchtime now, and you come eat with me at the restaurant and you will not be able to say that again."

At the table in the restaurant, after we gave our orders, I said: "Brother Vaughan, I belong to the P. B."

He said: "What's that?"

I said: "The public blessing society. Will you ask the blessing?"

"Right here?" he asked, startled.

"Yes," I said, "and out loud."

Quickly he said: "O Lord, thank you for what we are about to receive. Amen."

Then he turned to me and said: "Ain't that faith—asking God to bless what you ain't seen?"

Thinking of Chester and the First Baptist Church, I remember that I wanted Chester to have an old-fashioned revival meeting. So the church, in conference assembled, voted to have such a fourteen-day meeting, and asked me to do the preaching.

I prayed morning, noon, and night for this meeting—even as did my Lady Lee. Some interested men of the church got the old tent that young Gypsy Smith had used in the county-wide crusade.

At the beginning, movement was slow. Then it picked up and crowds came each night. Sweet gospel singing prevailed, yearning, now yawning seemed to prevail. Many accepted my statement that if an auto had as many useless parts as the average Baptist church, it would not run down hill—and determined to be useful. Some—in the congregation were booze drinkers—acknowledged that what I said was true—that booze was as bad as poison and sewerage in a family drinking fountain, as bad as strychnine in the baby's milk bottle, as bad as poison ivy for a bride's bouquet, as bad as a rattlesnake in a kindergarten, as bad as a mad dog on a children's playground, as bad as a rapist in a girls' dormitory, as bad as a maniac wielding a razor in an old folks' home.

Some resented what I said in condemnation of the modern dance and card-playing and divorce. Some, who claimed to be scholarly, rather violently criticized me for being "unscientific" and a "back number" when I declared that evolution believed in and taught as a fact and not a theory, had changed, caricatured, cursed, and crucified the minds of many. Quite a number "got mad with me" when I declared that Christians who did not pay God his tenth were robbers or thieves.

Many arrows of criticism were shot at me during those days—and some of the arrows were tipped with poison. But there were many verbal bouquets of praise and encouragement given to me, too.

Twice a great hindrance to the nightly services came. Twice did a thunderstorm rip the tent and blow it to the ground. But many good women came with huge needles and strong thread and sewed up the torn tent—and not all were Baptist women. Some Methodists, Presbyterians, and Episcopalians joined and worked diligently with the "sewing party." And the men raised the tent and arranged it properly. Grateful memories I hold in my heart today of these dear and diligently determined women and men.

During those days, alienated husbands and wives were reconciled, broken homes were mended, icy attitudes were melted, critical tongues were tamed, restitutions were made, unbelievers became believers, and God was glorified. Many united with the church, many by baptism upon confession of faith. I, as did many others, had a heart joy ever fascinating and never wearisome.

One was great joy because of the conversion of Baxter Crenshaw, a young man of twenty who, for some sort of crime, was serving a sentence on the county chain gang—when all the men in the gang wore striped clothes.

Baxter, during the second week of the meeting, wrote me a hard-to-read note, telling me he wanted to come in to be in the revival meeting and maybe, he said, "learn how to be saved." In response, I went out and had a talk with the superintendent of the chain gang and asked him if he would give Baxter permission to come in to the tent meeting. He gave permission, provided I would come and get him myself and bring him back myself by eleven at night. He said, "But he will have to wear his chain gang clothes." Though I knew this would make Baxter conspicuously uncomfortable, I agreed.

The chain gang was six miles at that time from Chester as to location. I drove out one day about sundown and the superintendent of the chain gang brought out Baxter, and turned him over to my care.

I talked to Baxter about Jesus on our drive from the chain gang location to the assembly place under the tent. He wanted, because of the big striped clothes, to sit on the back seat. I told him that would be appropriate, but that I wanted him to listen to my sermon.

I preached that night a simple sermon on how a sinner can be saved. The invitation was given while the choir sang "Just As I Am." Baxter came forward, his chain gang garb looking very vivid amid the lights under the tent. Baxter confessed his faith in Christ. I took him back to the chain gang location by 11:00 P.M., and I saw the guards put the chains around his ankles and fasten them to part of the iron bed on which Baxter had slept every night for seven months. He was among those whom I baptized in the river. He gave no sign that he had any interest to escape from me or the chain gang superintendent.

After he left the chain gang, Baxter dropped by to see me at my home and expressed thanks for what I had done for him as to body and soul. He said he believed God wanted him to be a preacher.

Baxter started to school to get an education and to be a preacher. Tuberculosis laid hold upon him and sent him to the sanatarium in Oteen, North Carolina, and in a few months, to the grave.

Without consulting anybody, I announced at one night service that those who came for baptism would be baptized on Sunday afternoon in the Sandy River.

Next morning, the deacons, concerned and courteous, came to the parsonage and seriously asked me to renounce the baptism announcement. I think they had—good men all—had denouncement in their hearts if not on their tongues, for my announcement.

One deacon said: "Pastor, that will be a circus-like scene—and will be the occasion of behavior unbecoming."

Expressing appreciation for their concern and courtesy, I said: "Brethren, I got the announcement about the baptism in the river from God and from Jesus who was baptized in the Jordan River."

Then I called upon them to pray silently while I prayed aloud for God's guidance in the baptism in the Sandy River.

During the meeting, the Chester drunk, "Old Bob Ingram," was saved and quit the bottle. The manager of a soft-drink manufacturing plant was saved.

Many others—children, young men and women, and some older folks—were converted.

The Sunday afternoon for the baptism came. At the morning service in the big tent, the chairman of the deacons said to me: "Preacher, I love you, but I am afraid about the baptism in the river."

I said: "Beloved, leave it to me. I will handle all matters. God will help me."

That afternoon, according to the report given by *The Chester Reporter,* over five thousand people were present on the banks and in the vicinity of the river. A choir of about a hundred and fifty voices was on the bank near the spot selected for the baptismal ordinance.

I got on the top of a Ford truck and asked the people to be quiet. I said: "We are to witness one hundred and twenty burials this afternoon. At a burial in a cemetery, nobody laughs or talks or misbehaves, and I quoted Colossians 2:12: "Buried with him in baptism."

I quoted Romans 6:3-4: "Know ye not, that so many of us as were baptized into Jesus Christ were baptized into his death? Therefore we are buried with him by baptism into death: that like as Christ was raised up from the dead by the glory of the Father, even so we also should walk in newness of life."

I said that there should be no voices heard except my voice and the choir. I baptized one hundred and twenty—taking over two hours to do so. There were some tears, but no talking. A sacred hush was on the riverside throng when "old Bob Ingram" and Baxter Crenshaw, a chain gang young man, walked into the river and were baptized.

After the "big baptism," as the administration of the ordinance to one hundred and twenty was dubbed by some, I baptized twenty-two people in the baptistry in the church house that night. Joy that bordered on consternation was in the heart of many.

The deacon who had expressed doubt as to the misbehavior and "cutting up" that might prevail at the river, came to me and said: "Well, pastor, I must give you praise. I have heard more talking and have seen more bad conduct at a funeral than I saw this afternoon, down by the riverside."

That night, I could hardly go to sleep, thinking of the one hundred and forty two whom I had baptized that Lord's day. That was the largest number I ever baptized in any one day.

Taking you back to think of the Chester pastorate, I tell you of my "encounter" with a lady who was a member of the church choir—a sweet-spirited young woman, Miss Vivian Gregory.

Her seat in the choir was right behind my chair on tne pulpit platform. She claimed to be a singer. But I and many others did not agree with her evaluation of her singing ability.

Sometimes—or it so seemed to me—she sang tenor, touched on the baritone and bass, and mixed the alto with soprano tones.

I said to "Miss Daisy," the organist: "Do you know what is wrong with our choir?"

"Oh, yes," she said.

"Why don't you ask Miss Vivian out?"

"Not I. I don't want a hundred folks on my neck making efforts to cut my throat. She has more friends than anybody in town."

I went to Professor Brockman, superintendent of the public schools of Chester and of the Sunday School. I said: "Buck, do you know what is wrong with our choir?"

"Yes, I've been knowing a long time," he said soberly.

"Why don't you ask Miss Vivian out?" I asked.

"Not I. I don't want folks troubling me about such a matter." He showed that he would adamantly oppose any further urging from me.

I went to Mr. Irvin, editor and publisher of the town newspaper. I said: "Brother Irvin, do you know what is wrong with our choir?"

"Oh, yes, and I am not the only one who knows."

"Why don't you talk to Miss Vivian and kindly ask her to leave the choir?"

"Not I," he said, "she has many friends, and I don't want to lose any subscribers to my paper. And I would if I did what you ask of me."

I went to Jake Perkins, chariman of the deacons, and one of the best Christians I have ever known. Sitting in his office, I asked: "Brother Jake, do you know what is the matter with our choir and the discords in it?"

"Yes," he said, "I've been knowing that for five years."

"Why don't you ask Miss Vivian out. You are chairman of the deacons, and nobody believes you would do anything wrong."

"Well," he said, "you are the pastor. Why don't *you* ask her out?"

Quickly I said, "I will." And I did.

It was this way. I went to the department store where Miss Vivian was an employee. When I entered the store, she had a bolt of cloth on the counter and was measuring and cutting off a few yards for a customer.

She saw me, and she said: "See you in a minute, Preacher, as soon as I get through with my customer."

She wrapped up the cloth and the customer left.

Miss Vivian said: "Now, preacher, what can I do for you?"

"Do you really want to know, Miss Vivian?" I asked.

"Sure," she said.

I screwed my courage to the sticking place, and said: "I want you to get out of the choir!"

Shocked, she looked straight into my eyes and asked a simple "Why?"

"Because you can't sing," I said.

She asked with a startled vehemence: "Do you think that will help the church?"

"Yes," I said.

"Well, I want to help the church and you, Dr. Lee, and I'm willing to do anything right that will help my church."

Then she pointed her finger at me and said: "But I tell you one thing, you'll never stop me from singing in the congregation."

I told her I would never interfere with that

Before the day was over, it was all over town—with long tongues spreading it abroad that the pastor had asked Miss Vivian out of the choir. Some, with criticism of me, declared that Miss Vivian and her folks would not be found in the First Baptist Church after my "cruelty" to this young woman.

But Miss Vivian hushed much of the gossip, declaring with kind remarks about her pastor that she was always willing to do anything that would help her church and her pastor.

Next Sunday morning, Miss Vivian's seat in the choir was vacant. But Miss Vivian was in the congregation singing lustily and gladly though those who were close to her wondered if she really was singing.

Two years after this choir episode, I wrote some of the young people that I would pass through Chester on a midnight train and would be glad to see some of the young people, if they would come to the railroad station. About two hundred of the dear young people were there. Miss Vivian was in the crowd, standing on the outer edge of the crowd. I saw her. I waved my hand at her and shouted: "Hey, Miss Vivian! Are you singing in the choir now?"

"No", she said, "but you ought to hear me in the congregation!"

That choir event created an impression for good in all of Chester.

Miss Vivian's sweetness of spirit, her refusal to criticize me, her refusal to have her feelings hurt, her continued faithful service, her hushing the mouths of those who criticized me, taught many how real Christians ought to live and be willing to take hurts for the good of the church.

Let me just say here that I came out better with Miss Vivian than did one pastor with a nasal-voiced tenor whom the choir members and the choir director wanted out of the choir but did not have the courageous tact and tactful courage to ask him out. So the choir master put the "dirty work" off on the pastor.

The pastor asked this man to come by the office. And there the pastor told him it would be good thing for him to leave the choir.

"Why, pastor," he asked with the nasal tones in his voice, "I have been in the choir for four years."

"Yes, I know, but I heard three people say you cannot sing."

"Aw! That aint nothin'! I heard fifty-six people say you can't preach!"

So!

5.
Ministry in the Crescent City

I was "fresh and green" off the farm. I knew no kind of work except farm work of various kinds. The only city I had ever seen before I landed in New Orleans was Charlotte, North Carolina.

In my young years, it was customary for a son to stay with his father until he was twenty-one years old. Then he was his own man and was no longer under obligation "to stay at home until twenty-one." I stayed with my father on the farm until Friday before I was twenty-one the following week.

I had heard that there was "good pay" for workers on the Panama Canal. I decided to go to Panama to earn enough money to enter the preparatory school and then to college. I had no money.

I borrowed $150 from the president of the Fort Mill bank and bought my ticket to New Orleans, leaving enough money to buy my steamer ticket from New Orleans to Panama. The passenger train, because of a wreck ahead, was delayed five hours. That caused me to miss connections with the steamship.

That was the first time I saw any of the city of New Orleans—in November, 1907—a big city which, with its gong-clanging street cars and cabs and multitudes of people hurrying and scurrying in all directions, confused me. I knew little of "city folks and city doings." I knew nothing of a bathroom or a commode or electric fixtures or coffee shops and restaurants.

I made my way in bewilderment to the ticket office of the United Fruit Company and there bought my steamer ticket to Panama. That left me with empty pockets.

Multitudes of faces saw I, but not one that I knew. I passed the doors of oyster bars and restaurants, but I had no money to buy a meal. I walked into the St. Charles hotel and stood amazed at the beauty and I was entranced as I listened to an orchestra playing. All the time I was carrying my suit case. Some of the uniformed porters in the hotel gazed at me, and two laughed.

On the street I passed rooming houses, but I had no room and no money to pay for one. And it would be a week before the steamship left for Panama.

In the 1040 block of Canal Street was a rooming house. I walked into the little corridor before the front door and knocked on the door. A little lady with a kind face came to the door, a towel over her left arm.

"Why did you not buzz the bell?" she asked. I knew nothing about buzzing bells in a city boarding house. At home we knocked on doors or shouted "hello" loudly to let folks know we were there and would like to talk.

"I didn't know how," I said.

Then I told her my plight—that I was on my way to Panama to work to get some money to go to school. And I showed her my ticket. Then I said: "If you will take me in and give me a room and something to eat, I'll get a job and pay you back next Friday."

With a glance at me and my dirty hat and suitcase, she said: "You are from the country, aren't you?"

"Yes, ma'am" I said.

"Are you a Christian?" she asked earnestly.

"Yes, ma'am, but not as good a one as I want to be."

"Is your mother living?" she asked quietly.

"Yes, ma'am."

"I'll take you and trust you," she said. "Come with me."

She took me up two flights of staris to the third floor of the big old boarding house and showed me a very small room with a narrow bed, a cracked mirror, and a wash stand. On the wash stand was a little bowl in which was a cake of fragrant Cashmere Bouquet soap. That little dish and cake of soap make me homesick. That was the kind of soap we put in the pastor's room when he spent the night at our house. We never used much soap, but strong lye soap made by my mother.

There was a bathroom on the floor, used by all the boarders on that floor. Someone said about a room, "It was so small you had to get out in the hall to change your mind."

I and my dirty hat and suitcase had a home anyway. Next morning, I went down to the wharf at the river end of Canal Street and got a job carrying bananas from the freighter to the railroad fruit cars. I carried bunches of bananas fifteen hours a day and made enough money to pay my landlady late Friday afternoon, and I had several dollars over which would help me when I got to Panama.

If that day my landlady had told me that in fifteen years I would be in New Orleans again and pastor of the First Baptist Church with a salary and a home, I would have thought she was talking utter nonsense or speaking as one gripped by a nightmare of a disordered brain.

But in fifteen years such was so, because, in June 1922, the First Baptist Church of New Orleans extended a unanimous call for me to become their pastor. My answer by wire to the unanimous call was as follows:

For my decision read consecutively: 1 Thess. 3:11: "Now God himself and our Father, and our Lord Jesus Christ, direct our way unto you." 2 John 12: "Having many things to write unto you, I would not write with paper and ink: but I trust to come unto you, and speak face to face, that our joy may be full." Romans 15:29: "And I am sure that, when I come unto you, I shall come in the fulness of the blessing of the gospel of Christ." 2 Thess. 3:4: "And we have confidence in the Lord touching you, that ye both do and will do the things which we command you." Phil. 1:22-26: "But if I live in the flesh, this is the fruit of my labour: Yet what I shall choose I wot not. For I am in a strait betwixt two, having a desire to depart, and to be with Christ; which is far better: Nevertheless to abide in the flesh is more needful for you. And having this confidence I know that I shall abide and continue with you all for your furtherance and joy of faith; that your rejoicing may be more abundant in Jesus Christ for me by my coming to you again." Romans 15:30: "Now I beseech you, brethren, for the Lord Jesus Christ's sake, and for love of the Spirit, that ye strive together with me in your prayers to God for me." Read this to the church assembled.

On Sunday, September 17, 1922, fifteen years after I had carried bananas at the wharf at the river-end of Canal Street, I began my ministry at the First Baptist Church. There were seven hundred and fifty-eight members. The Sunday school was less than three hundred in numbers. My salary was four thousand dollars a year.

When I got my first check from Brother Arnold, treasurer, I thought of the day fifteen years before when I got pay for the loads of bananas I had carried for five days, getting money to pay my benevolent little landlady.

Tuesday night, October 3, the church gave a reception for me and my wife and little daughter. Dr. W. W. Hamilton, who became the president of the Southern Baptist Convention in 1941-42, gave an address of welcome on behalf of the Baptists of the state of Louisiana. Dr. W. A. Jordan brought a similar message from the Baptists of New Orleans. Dr. B. H. DeMent, president of the New Orleans Baptist Bible Institute, which later became known as the New Orleans Baptist Theological Seminary, gave a brief address representing the Institution.

In later months DeMent could say of me and I could say of DeMent what David said of Jonathan: "My brother . . . very pleasant hast thou been to me; thy love to me was wonderful, passing the love of women" (2 Sam. 1:26). There was an address made by Dr. J. T. Christian who represented the members of the church.

Grateful to God for his goodness, I set to work. I resolved to visit the homes of the entire church membership. It took me three months to make these pastoral visits.

I projected plans which would bring about increased attendance in Sunday School and along with that, strengthen the quality of the teaching. This effort was rewarded with quick success. Within a few months the Sunday School attendance doubled, new leadership was pressed into service, and the challenge was issued for those in places of leadership to train themselves for effective service.

I preached that our church had a corporate stewardship of time, talent, and treasure. I taught the members that they made their greatest contribution to the causes of Christ when they came to grips with real sorrow, real hatred, real sin.

I visited many people and many places in New Orleans—offices, homes, hospitals, schools. I worked night and day—teaching, studying, preaching, visiting.

I took on too much in the matter of work. My body which, fifteen years before was strong enough to carry bananas in huge bunches, became weak. The wealth of good health departed—I had to leave, and I spent ten weeks in a sanatorium, absent from my pulpit. But God restored me, and I left the sanatorium for the pulpit rejoicing in restoration of health and strength.

I would have to have the ability to put an ocean into a gallon bucket to speak of all the blessings God showered upon the First Baptist Church in New Orleans during my pastorate. During those days many verbal brickbats were thrown at me. Some of them bruised and hurt. But some of the bouquets outweighed in worth all the brickbats. Here for example:

James H. Tharpe, chairman of the deacons, wrote the *Baptist Courier* in South Carolina these words: "Our church has not much wealth and the task was thought to be impossible, but our pastor's faith is full, and fortified by unfailing answers to every prayer."

Prof. H. T. Cox, one of my teachers at Furman University, wrote: "Be humble, earnest, willing to stay or go where he wills. I told you once that you had at that time within you the making of a great preacher. Somehow or other the Lord helps me to form correct judgments regarding college boys. The great preacher is revealing himself. Let him come modestly, but powerfully, to the front."

Dr. Ellis Fuller, later president of the southern Baptist Theological Seminary in Louisville, Kentucky, wrote: "Lee, I could not if I had words, congratulate you sufficiently for your great achievements in that city."

The Baptist Message gave me these verbal flowers after I addressed the Louisiana Baptist State Convention: "Dr. Robert G. Lee of New Orleans swept the convention up to 'seventh heaven' with a masterpiece address Thursday morning. It was good to have been there. Those who left before the convention adjourned sustained a distinct loss by failing to hear Lee. . . . Lee preached on social service. He was as fine as I ever heard. I took out my handkerchief and cried as he told those wonderful stories."

I held some revival meetings in other cities while in New Orleans. One of particular interest was the one at the First Baptist Church, Shreveport, where the distinguished Dr. M. E. Dodd was pastor. There were one hundred seventy additions to the church—one hundred four for baptism upon confession of faith. During this meeting, Huey Long, who became governor of Louisiana, placed his membership by letter in the church.

During my years in New Orleans, other churches sought me for pastor. In 1924 the Grove Avenue Baptist Church, Richmond, Virginia, wanted me to come and succeed Dr. Len G. Broughton. A pulpit committee made up of *fifty members!* was willing with my assent to place my name before the church. But I could not give my approval.

The First Baptist Church, Beaumont, Texas, contacted me, and a Mr. Carrol, rich oil man, chairman of the pulpit committee, begged and begged me to become pastor at Beaumont.

Columbus Avenue Baptist Church, Waco, Texas, also wanted me for pastor in 1925. But I could not believe God wanted me to leave New Orleans.

I remember my third anniversary as pastor in New Orleans—in September, 1925. On that third anniversary, there were thirty-three additions to the church. Records reveal that up to this point there had been 909 additions to the church. Attendance in all the organizations was at an all-time high. The church's gifts were higher from 1922-1925 than they had been from 1914-1922. In appreciation the church gave me and Mrs. Lee a new automobile.

While at the First Baptist Church, New Orleans, my mother died— May 4, 1923. When I went home for the funeral, the sunshine seemed filled with shadows, the songs of the mockingbirds seemed to hold dirges. Still was the heart of the wonderful woman whose first prayer for me was that I would become a preacher.

In New Orleans, I baptized into the membership of the church over one hundred Catholics—among them a Mr. Harry Smith, president of an oil refining company, the Gulf, I believe.

Four other events in New Orleans I relate. One was with reference to Nellie Dawson Wright—seventeen-year-old widow of William E. Wright.

One Sunday night I preached on the "Case of Little Nell." Wright had been shot down by the police in a gun battle and his wife, Nell, was being held as an accomplice to some of his crimes. I paid a visit to Nell in her jail cell. I came to certain conclusions on the basis of the interview. I spoke of the girl as being "a flower of girlhood captured by the strange wooing of human cactus, a sparrow who accepted the love of a night hawk, a modest maid ensnared by the bold daring of a master criminal."

Stressing the importance of home influence, I cited Bill Wright's crime as an example of evil doing. Concerning "little Nell" I said: "If I were on the jury, they would have to wait for the ants to carry me out before I would convict little Nell." It was my opinion that Nell should be sent back to her home, and then rebuild her shattered life.

The New Orleans papers reported my remarks which aroused the district attorney, Judge Marr. The latter claimed that because of public hysteria, a fair trial could not be held in Orleans Parish. I was served a subpoena to appear as a witness before Judge O'Donnell.

District Attorney Marr said: "I have always been taught that the church is for law and order and this is the first time that I have heard a minister delivering a sermon that would have the effect of bringing about a disregard of law and order." I did not retreat one inch under the attack of the district attorney. I said: "In football language, Judge Marr was way off side! He pulled a green one. With no apology to anybody for what I have preached, with emphasized reiteration of all my sermons, I declare that my sermon, everything in it, would prove Judge Marr's accusation and public raillery against me to be nonsensically awry, diabolically unfair, blindly lopsided, and sordidly undignified."

I continued: "As a minister I have the right, in the land of free speech, to speak my convictions based on the ground of a careful interview without being accused by Judge Marr of preaching 'anarchy and revolution.' Such accusations are unbecoming to our district attorney. I have never heard of an argument for a change of venue accompanied by such unjust, unfair, cheap nightmares. Judge Marr can attack me in court, but he cannot muzzle me in the pulpit. Let him hear my five-minute reply to him Sunday night from my pulpit, and over the radio. Every visitor is an honored guest in our church. Judge, you subpoened me to court, I invite you to church. How about it?"

One statement that Judge Marr made caused indignation on my part. He suggested that I should study the Bible more thoroughly. This brought a rejoinder from me: "I would not be surprised if I knew my Bible as well as Judge Marr knows law."

Judge O'Donnell denied the application for a change of venue and Nell was returned to her family. The decision met with public approval. "They make me tired," remarked Clarence Darrow, Chicago's noted criminal lawyer who defended Nathan Leopold and Richard Loeb and who was in New Orleans to debate St. Clair Adams, when asked his opinion of the prosecution of Nellie Dawson Wright.

I think of Katherine Wilson. I received a brief letter, signed "Katherine Wilson," asking me to come and give "a girl all wrong" some counsel and "point her the way to God." The number of the house and street given was 1308 Tulane Avenue. With purpose to "point to God" this girl, I went, but I failed to win her to faith in Christ, even though she was "almost persuaded."

About two weeks after my visit to this young woman who had thrown away in Folly's Court and Carnal Pleasure's Mart the gold of her youth, I found the following write-up in a New Orleans newspaper:

Police seek slayer of pretty woman shot after quarrel.
"The wages of sin is death!"

It's an old, old story. Old as humanity. New as the morning records of the police department that register the report: "No new developments in the search for John Pleasant Harris, 35, ex-convict, sought for the murder of Katherine Wilson, 28, of 1308 Tulane Ave."

"The wages of sin is death."

In some other world than this Katherine Wilson, if the dead know anything, knows this today. In the dark hours of Sunday morning before dawn, clad in her dainty pink silk negligee, she knelt in the street car tracks of Tulane Avenue, pleading for her life. Only a few feet away was the Criminal Courts Building, housing the police headquarters and the uniformed men whose duty it is to enforce the law that New Orleans' Cabaret Belt flouts.

Over her, insane with rage, stood Harris. From the windows of police headquarters could be seen the flash as his pistol spat flame, and the young woman fell, shot through the neck.

"The wages of sin is death."

So ends the tragedy of Katherine Wilson. Under the large glass cover of the dining room table in the apartment of 1308 Tulane Avenue were a score or more of little mottoes clipped from magazines and from newspapers. Short poems, songs, and little articles are in the collection.

Among them, these stand out:

"Shoot straight in life as you would in forest, field, or target; your aim is not enough—hit that's what counts."

"The man who hesitates is lost and so is the women who doesn't."

"What's a vamp?"

"Those we love."

"Did you ever sit and ponder?"

"No woman feels so securely in love with one man that she does not keep an eye out for another one."

"Kiss or miss!"

"Say it With Music."

"Summer friends fall off like leaves when the frosts of misfortune come."

"I never knew."

"A hop fiend's dream."

"The little red God."

But there's one that didn't appear there—though Katherine Wilson stands as one of the eternal monuments of its truth. She could have heard it from any one of the score of pulpits where sermons were preached that Sabbath in the early hours of which she died, screaming for mercy: "The wages of sin is death."

While pastor in New Orleans, I went back to South Carolina for a week of revival preaching. On my way back to New Orleans, I had five hours between trains in Atlanta. Wearied with a week of preaching and "being company" in many homes, I got a room at the Piedmont Hotel for four hour's rest.

While I was in bed the room telephone rang. A voice said: "Are you Mister Lee?"

"Yes," I said.

"You *must* come down," said a man's voice, deep, gruff, rough.

"Who is this who tells me I *must* come down. There is only one *must* I obey, and that is my wife's," I said jokingly.

"*I* said you must," the man answered. "A man in trouble says you *must.*"

I dressed and went down to the lobby. I had the man paged. He came to me, his whole body a-tremble, his fingers on both hands biting down into the palms of his hands.

"I took a shot on you," he said, "I saw your name on the hotel register and saw you are from New Orleans. I used to live there, and I thought since I *once* lived there and you *now* live there you would listen to me!"

I said: "Sit down here." I pointed to a settee. We both sat down.

I asked: "Are you a Christian?"

"Christian," he said, almost with a snarl. "I'm just out of the Federal pen two days, and the little bit of money they gave me is gone! And I am hungry. And I got to have some money, and if I don't get it one way, I am going to get it another! You got any?"

The way he looked at me I hoped I had some.

I asked: "How much do you want?"

"I don't want as much as I *want*," he almost shouted, "I want as much as I *need* to get something to eat and get me a job. Can you let me have forty dollars?"

"I don't have forty dollars in my pocket," I said, "but I know Mr. Dehoney at the Southern States Insurance Company and I can get the forty from him. Wait here until I get back."

I got the forty dollars from Mr. Dehoney as a loan. When I got back, I handed it to the man. He grabbed it with fingers and started out. I put my hand on his shoulder, and said: "Wait a minute! I want to introduce you to my friend."

"*Who* is he? *Where* is he?" he asked nervously.

"His name is Jesus, and he is everywhere," I said.

He sat down and I told him as hurriedly as I could about Jesus and what Jesus would do for him *if* only he would accept him as Savior and have him as a friend.

The man listened, and then sprang to his feet.

"That sounds good! That sounds good!" he said loudly. "But I am hungry!" He stuffed the forty dollars worth of bills in his pocket and went swiftly out the door to the street.

I prayed: "O Lord, cause that poor man to know that more than I had time to tell him about Jesus is so."

About two years later, I preached from my pulpit on the subject "Christ Receiveth Sinful Men." When I gave the invitation, down the aisle of the church came a man nicely dressed and intelligent of face. He grabbed me by the hand and held on to it.

He looked straight into my eyes: "Preacher, do you know me?" he asked with a faint smile and with great seriousness. I looked at him a moment.

"Why, yes," I said, "You are my forty-dollar man."

"That's right," he said. He sat down on the front seat. I sat down beside him. Some others came to join the church, and one of the deacons greeted them.

"Preacher," said the man, "I came to find out that more than you had time to tell me about Jesus is so—what you told me in the hotel lobby in Atlanta on the darkest day of my life. Jesus saved me in St. Louis, and I came down here to tell you so and to let the hands that gave me forty dollars on such a dark day of my life baptize me."

I was amazed and happy. Then he put his mouth close to my ear and whispered: "You'll not have to tell the people about the gray walls, will you?" He had reference to the walls of the Federal Prison in Atlanta.

"No," said I. "It's none of their business if Jesus and you have settled matters."

"We've settled all matters," he said, with a sigh of relief.

We received him as a believer who asked baptism. He spent a week in New Orleans. He ate at the table in our home. He held my little daughter on his knee and told her a fairy story.

The next Sunday night I baptized him in beautiful baptism. And nobody but he and my wife and God knew that I was putting under the water in Christian baptism a man who had spent twelve years behind the walls of a Federal prison.

Speaking of baptism, reminds me that a French sailor and a German sailor who had fought against each other in World War I were in the baptistry at the same time one Sunday night. Those who were enemies and fought to kill each other became brothers in Christ Jesus, justified freely by God's grace as it is in Christ Jesus.

Yes, God did some great things in the First Baptist Church of New Orleans, Louisiana.

Though I had spoken four times, and though I had given forty minutes to a wedding and had administered the ordinance of baptism one Sunday night, I felt that I must be at my office early. I asked Mrs. Watson, my secretary, to meet me there at 7:30. She did, being there before I arrived. When I came into my office, she came in and said: "A young lady has been waiting to see you."

"Who is she?" I asked.

"I do not know. She did not tell me her name; and I felt I should not ask her. But she was waiting here when I came."

I said: "Send her in."

In a moment, there walked into my office a young woman who was making an effort to be calm, efforts perceptible at once. I arose to greet her, and asked her to be seated. She was, I judged, about eighteen years of age. Extravagantly dressed, with a huge white fur neckpiece around her neck and shoulders. A frilly little hat perched perilously on the side of her head. One hand, her left, was gloved, and she held a right glove in her left hand. There was a haunting look about her eyes and a slight frown on her brow, and she looked as though smiles had been strangers to her face for a long time. And when she spoke, it seemed that laughter had been an alien matter to her mouth.

"Last night I heard you preach, but I was not in the auditorium." She appeared to be somewhat old beneath her mask of rouge, her youth tainted with viciousness.

"I am sure you were not" I said lightly, "for had you been here wearing that I would have seen you."

I smiled. She appeared to be somewhat more serious, and seemed slightly provoked.

"But I stood on the corner of Delachaise, just outside, and heard you preach. I hated you and all you said until you said that God accepts a surrendered desert. And I knew that I must see you. I have no father or mother; no brothers; no sisters that I know of. Would you let me talk to you as though you were my father and loved me, my mother and understood me? I am a human desert."

"Yes," I said, "all you tell me shall be kept as a sacred secret."

Then she talked with me—at first in a subdued voice I could hardly hear, as though she were afraid others would hear her. Sympathetically and intently did I listen as she, with a hesitancy that bordered, at first, on distrust, verbally turned the dirty pages of a life of sordid shame and sin. It was like watching one empty out a garbage can on the parlor floor. It was like standing near a smoking fire and getting smoke that hurt in one's eyes.

After she had finished the sordid recital, she looked at me as one crying for help and yet as one who would be defiant should I not help; as one struggling in a muddy sewerage river grasping for the last plank that drifted slowly by; as one in despair calling and getting no answer of hope. Her words shocked me. My heart was in my throat. She looked at me with eyes that burned strangely, as one tired of sin, tired of life, tired and distrustful of everybody.

"Do you think there is any chance for a girl like me to get back, to get out of the ditch, and on the road again? Will God—*will* God—accept my surrendered desert and make it blossom? You said he would. Is it so?" Her words were ominous with distrust and fear—and penitence. My lips seemed to freeze to my teeth.

The recital of things she had done seemed to daze me into speechlessness. I did not, could not, speak at first. She took my silence for reluctance and cried out, almost shrieked out, as though she wanted all the world to know: "If you don't think so, if what you said last night is a lie, then you'll read of 'em fishing my body out of the river tomorrow, if they can find it!" Her voice had in it the wail that bordered on a snarl. She stood to her feet and was gripping the corner of my desk with trembling fingers. Her whole body was a-quiver.

Then I spoke. I told her that all I said the night before was so—that Christ would be far more than words could tell to all who with repentance toward God and faith in Christ surrendered to him. I told her that Christ would accept her surrendered desert and restore the years the locusts had eaten and make her, though smutty from contact with the devil's pots, to be as "a dove covered with silver, and her feathers with yellow gold" (Ps. 68:13).

To come quickly to the end of a darkened road, I will simply say that she accepted Christ, knelt in prayer, and promised to "see me again." As she went out the back door from my office, she took off the costly white fur neckpiece and dropped it in the rubbish can just outside the door.

Later, I baptized her—nobody, not even my secretary, knowing of her terrible sin, knowing nothing of her having been the dirty toy of dirtier men for three years.

These unworthy hands of mine baptized her. These eyes saw her smile as I put her face slowly under water. Next day she telephoned me that she was "leaving town" to start anew.

Five years later—in another city—she came to my house with a young man. She stood before me at the marriage hour in our home, a fine young man beside her, a young man whose life, while in his teens, was one of awful sin. He, too, had been redeemed. Both of them told me they were getting married "without any secrets," that they had opened all the pages of both books when they talked of marriage and became engaged. They said that they had forgiven what needed to be forgiven in each other and that they were forgetting the past, starting over in beginning life together.

I saw them as they left our little home. They stopped on the edge of the sidewalk and looked up at the stars, as though they were praying to God; and then they kissed, and went away arm in arm, heart to heart, hand in hand, soul to soul.

I know where they live now. Their surrendered deserts have become gardens of the Lord. And their little children are beautiful flowers in the garden.

6.
Back in South Carolina

From New Orleans, Louisiana, on the Mississippi, to Charleston, South Carolina, "the place where the Ashley and Cooper rivers meet to form the Atlantic Ocean," I went in 1925.

I was thirty-nine years of age when I became pastor of the Citadel Square Baptist Church, a church whose history dates back to 1854. Through the years the church had been recognized as one of the leading churches, not only of South Carolina, but of the Southern Baptist Convention. Among my predecessors were Dr. E. C. Dargan—once president of the Southern Baptist Convention.

When he died, Dargan was buried in Chicago. During the sessions of the Southern Baptist Convention in Chicago, I left presiding over the Convention afternoon session to the vice-president and went to the cemetery with some other Baptist leaders, and held a memorial service at Dr. Dargan's grave.

Other former pastors of the church were Dr. David M. Ramsey, who became president of Greenville Woman's College, Greenville, South Carolina; Dr. Howard Lee Jones; and Dr. C. C. Coleman.

I am not boasting. but my willingness to work and my determination to make of myself the best pastor and preacher I was capable of being helped me to work many hours a day. I believed, as did my Lady Lee, that with God's help the impossible would become the possible.

Here is how my call to Citadel Square came about. When the congregation was left without a pastor upon the resignation of Dr. C. C. Coleman, my name was urged upon the pulpit committee by some who received information that it would be possible to move me from the First Baptist Church in New Orleans. The committee learned that it was highly probable that they could secure the services

(Top) Mr. and Mrs. David Ayers Lee, parents of Robert Greene Lee
(Bottom) The home where they were married on Christmas Eve, 1875

The cabin where Robert Greene Lee was born

Mother Lee's iron, scissors, and sewing basket

The old bell which used to ring out on the Lee farm

(Top left) The high chair where R. G. Lee once sat (Top right) Trunk where his mother packed her wedding clothes (Bottom left) The family hymnbook (Bottom right) Rabbit box built by young Lee

(Opposite page) This is an old picture of the First Baptist Church in Fort Mill, South Carolina. Lee was baptized there on August 15, 1898. On April 3, 1910, he was ordained by the church to the gospel ministry. Note the ordination certificate, upper right.

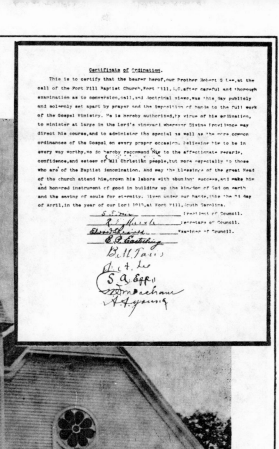

Certificate of Ordination.

This is to certify that the bearer herof, our Brother Robert G Lee, at the call of the Fort Mill Baptist Church, Fort Mill, S.C. after careful and thorough examination as to conversion, call, and doctrinal views, was this day publicly and solemnly set apart by prayer and the imposition of hands to the full work of the Gospel Ministry. He is hereby authorized, by virue of his ordination, to minister at large in the Lord's vineyard wherever Divine Providence may direct his course, and to administer the special as well as the more common ordinances of the Gospel on every proper occasion. Believing him to be in every way worthy, we do hereby recommend him to the affectionate regard, confidence, and esteem of all Christian people, but more especially to those who are of the Baptist denomination. And may the blessings of the great Head of the church attend him, crown his labors with abundant success, and make him and honored instrument of good in building up the kingdom of God on earth and the saving of souls for eternity. Given under our hands, this the 24 day of April, in the year of our Lord 1913, at Fort Mill, South Carolina.

S F Moir _____ President of Council.
R S Hartzle _____ Secretary of Council.
Elmer _____ Examiner of Council.
E P Cartuling
B M Faris
Ind A Le
S A Egg'll
Wm Pacham
A A young

Harmony
Baptist Church
Here I did my
first baptizing and
first administering
Lord's Supper.

Did my first baptizing her

The Rev. and Mrs. R. G. Lee at Edgefield, South Carolina (1918)

Opposite page—(Top) The Lima Baptist Church, Dr. Lee's first pastorate
(Middle left) Baptismal dressing rooms where he conducted his first baptismal
service at the Harmony Baptist Church (Middle right) The pulpit of Lima
Baptist Church (Bottom) The Harmony Church where Dr. Lee first officiated at
the ordinances

(Left) Dr. Lee and Dr. Ramsey Pollard, his successor at Bellevue, stand together. The occasion was the dedication of the Lee Memorial Garden, August 7, 1966. (Bottom left) The impressive auditorium building of the Bellevue Baptist Church, Memphis, Tennessee (Below) Dr. Lee with Mrs. Lee, who is now in heaven

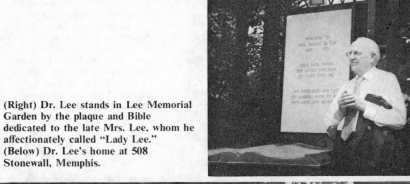

(Right) Dr. Lee stands in Lee Memorial Garden by the plaque and Bible dedicated to the late Mrs. Lee, whom he affectionately called "Lady Lee."
(Below) Dr. Lee's home at 508 Stonewall, Memphis.

(Above) Dr. Lee poses with his successors at Bellevue, Dr. Ramsey Pollard, center, and Dr. Adrian Rogers, right. (Below) Mrs. Hugh Dyer and Dr. Lee in front of the Memento House which is opened to the public on stated hours and by special arrangement.

of Dr. J. R. Hobbs, pastor of the First Baptist Church, Birmingham, Alabama. The church extended a call to Hobbs but he felt no inclination to accept. After this disappointment, the committee again thought in terms of me and their persistent efforts were rewarded with success.

I began my ministry in Charleston on Sunday, December 13, 1925. I was greeted with a large attendance in both Sunday School and church.

A city-wide welcome featured the Sunday evening service. A capacity audience enjoyed the program in the course of which Mayor Thomas P. Stoney made appropriate remarks on behalf of the city; Dr. Alexander Sprung spoke for the ministerial union; Dr. J. E. Bailey brought greetings from the sister Baptist churches of Charleston; and Mr. T. S. Wilbur spoke for the congregation. After these remarks, I responded.

One of the joys of the occasion was for me to have my gray-haired father present. In a remark to me that night, my father said: "Bob, I wish your ma could have been here. But I guess she's watching from above."

Two nights after the enthusiastic welcome, I attended my first deacons' meeting. There I discovered that the church was heavily, almost desperately, in debt in the amount of approximately $175,000—a monumental debt for that day. That night an agreement was reached to ask John P. Thomas to study possibilities for refinancing the church debt, a budget was adopted in the amount of $45,000 (the largest budget in the history of the church), the employment of a church secretary was authorized, and it was also recommended that the church have a bulletin printed each week.

On Wednesday, January 20, 1926, Mr. Thomas reported that the recent canvass of the membership had resulted in the securing of 814 pledges, totaling approximately $36,000. Thomas advised that while this was one of the largest amounts ever pledged for general purposes, it was short of expectations. He moved that the deacons continue their efforts to secure additional pledges. The motion carried.

There were times when I felt as though I had made the biggest mistake of my life in leaving New Orleans. Much of my time had to be given to finances. There were things I wanted, but conservative customs and lack of finances were a roadblock in the path of progress.

Today, I can affirm that I made no mistake. I would have no desire to rewrite the script of my Charleston ministry. There is a great love in my heart both for Charleston and for the people with whom I worked at Citadel Square. The disappointments experienced were blessings in disguise—they were part of life's discipline which would be helpful in later years.

In the Robert G. Lee biography by Dr. John E. Huss, we read:

While in Charleston, Dr. Lee played a game called "Boo" with his little daughter. Bula would tiptoe softly behind her father while he was studying and say "Boo." There were occasions when Lee would find his little girl absorbed in dressing her dolls, and he would slip quickly behind her and say "Boo."

One Sunday afternoon in the spring of 1926, Lee and his wife were sitting together in their living room and Lee asked, "Where is Bitsy?"

"Upstairs," Mrs. Lee replied.

Lee went upstairs and found her sitting on the floor, legs crossed, reading the Bible. He looked over her shoulder and saw that she was reading about the crucifixion of Christ in the nineteenth chapter of John. She was so intensely absorbed in her reading that she did not know her father was standing behind her and looking over her shoulder. Presently, she cried out: "Oh! They are going to kill Him! They are going to kill Him."

For once Lee did not say "Boo." He felt as though he were on holy ground. Bula was nine years of age and had experienced a deep concern about her salvation. Lee used this opportunity to read to her and to explain such verses from the Bible as John 1:12; 3:18; 3:26; Romans 10:9-13.

On Sunday evening, April 4, 1926, Bula walked down the aisle and made a profession of her faith in Christ while the congregation was singing, "Jesus, I Come"—the same hymn that was sung when Lee came to Jesus as a twelve-year-old boy in the revival at the Fort Mill Baptist Church. The selection of the hymn was not premeditated but was a coincidence.

So great and sweet to remember was the hour of the confession of Bula's faith that her father has framed, in the little Lee Memento House in Memphis, a picture of the church pew on which she sat—along with a picture of the spot in the lake where she was baptized. Bula was baptized Sunday afternoon, April 18th, at the lake in Hampton Park. An estimated audience of fifteen hundred persons witnessed the impressive baptism in this beautiful place.

The baptism of Bula must be considered one of the mountain top experiences in the lives of Dr. and Mrs. Lee.

I could not help but wonder how successful a revival effort would be—Charleston was different from any place I had ever been. Men such as George W. Truett, A. C. Dixon, D. L. Moody, and Mel Trotter had been to Charleston and had been disappointed because the revival fires did not burn as brightly as expected. But mixed up with my apprehension was a strong conviction that God could bring revival to Charleston, or any other place.

The meeting began as scheduled on Monday evening, October 25. I devoted the early messages to themes calculated to awaken and revive the membership. I challenged the church to meet God's conditions for a spiritual awakening as set forth in 2 Chronicles 7:14: "If my people, which are called by my name, shall humble themselves, and pray, and seek my face, and turn from their wicked ways, then will I hear from heaven, and will forgive their sin, and will heal their land." There were many who felt led during the first five nights to rededicate their lives to Christ. On Friday night there were six people who responded to the invitation—four of these came as candidates for baptism and two by letter.

On Sunday the revival flood gates were opened and during the day 33 people presented themselves for baptism, and 19 others came by letter or statement. Written in my diary are three words which sum up the joyful experience: "What a day!"

People responded every night during the second week, and then the following Sunday was another glorious day. When the final benediction was pronounced, the church received 91 persons for baptism and 53 in other ways—a total of 145 people for the two-week campaign. All of which proved that it is possible to have a revival anywhere.

At the end of the first year at Citadel Square, I sent all the members a letter outlining the progress that had been made. "One year ago I came to you under what I believed to be the will of God at your insistent call. You have given me a royal welcome. I have tried to do all things for the glory of God for the advancement of his kingdom. In this effort I have made many friends. I have also made some enemies. Doubtless, I have made some mistakes. I pray God will over-rule them for his glory."

During my first year at Citadel Square, the largest Sunday School attendance was 1,314, the largest prayer meeting was 500 folks. There were 362 additions to the church. I baptized 83 at one night service. I married 18 couples. I held 27 funeral services. I preached 107 sermons at Citadel Square and 133 elsewhere.

My diary shows that I made 2,455 visits. My first year the church gave to all causes $42,000. I furnished my own home, a rented house.

I wrote and had published my first book, *From Feet to Fathoms.* I dedicated this book to my mother.

To
My Mother
MRS. DAVID AYERS LEE
who said
that her first prayer
for me
was that I would be a preacher

My second book was *Lord, I Believe,* published by Broadman. In this book I wrote of the Bible miracles in the light of science. I asserted these truths: "The fundamental postulate of all rational thinking is the fact of God. I do not believe God is an impotent and puzzled bell-hop running up and down the corridors of the world house he designed by his omniscience and created by his omnipotence, having lost the keys to some of his own world house. God cannot be baffled or bothered or chained by the physical elements."

This book I dedicated to my wife with these words:

To
My Wife
BULA GENTRY LEE
WHOSE LOVING AND UNSELFISH COMPANIONSHIP HAS BEEN
TO ME A HIVE OF SWEETNESS, A FOUNTAIN OF JOY, A LAMP
OF LIGHT, A HARP OF MUSIC, AND A GARDEN OF ROSE

FLOWERS, ENABLING ME TO FACE LIFE'S PERILOUS
SITUATIONS WITH STRENGTH AND TO FIGHT LIFE'S BATTLES
WITH A BRAVER HEART.

I was invited to preach the baccalaureate sermon during the commencement exercises of the Citadel Military College—the West Point of the deep South, during the spring of 1927. It was requested that I deliver the sermon at Citadel Square Baptist Church. With joy and gratitude, I accepted.

A newspaper editor asked me to send him by mail the subject of my sermon. I did so, stating that my subject would be "Fleas and Dead Dogs." The editor made a courteous protest as to the subject, and said: "Mr. Lee, commencement time at college is one of the most elite occasions of the year. You don't mean you are going to use a cheap subject on such a notable and important occasion?"

"Yes", I replied, "that is my subject."

"Well, sir, you surely didn't find that subject in the Bible—the Book you say you preach" the editor said, seemingly somewhat nettled!

"If you will read 1 Samuel 24:14, you will find my subject." My text for the unusual subject was: "After whom is the king of Israel come out? after whom dost thou pursue? After a dead dog, after a flea."

I stayed with my subject and my text the Sunday morning of the baccalaureate sermon, and it was a spiritually effective service. The Commandant of the school was so delighted with the sermon that he had two thousand copies published for distribution.

I do not know if anyone would praise my service at Citadel Square. But the Sunday School had become the largest of all Sunday Schools in South Carolina. The church membership showed a substantial growth from about twelve hundred members to almost seventeen hundred members. The finances of the church increased appreciably—the church which at the beginning of my ministry was heavily in debt was now solvent. There was a marked increase in gifts to missions. In the span of exactly one hundred Sundays, I accomplished the work God sent me to do in Charleston.

The day came to say good-bye to Charleston—the beautiful, quaint and ancient city located on a narrow peninsula, to the double-spanned Cooper River Bridge, the archaic and lovely houses, the narrow, crooked streets, the stately church spires pointing toward heaven, King Street with its odd little shops, the historic battery, and the loveliest gardens in the world.

It was difficult to say good-bye. And I think of these words:

> Goodbye at the garden gate,
> Goodbye at the railroad station,
> Goodbye. 'tis a word we hate.
> Goodbye over all creation.

7.
My Life at Bellevue Baptist Church

I read in the Bible—Genesis 37:3—that Joseph, son of Jacob, was loved more by Jacob than all his children. "Now Israel loved Joseph more than all his children, because he was the son of his old age: and he made him a coat of many colours." Because of this, his brothers—all of them—hated Joseph.

Now Joseph had his dreams. He told his brothers what he had dreamed. "For, behold, we were binding sheaves in the field, and, lo, my sheaf arose, and also stood upright; and, behold, your sheaves stood round about, and made obeisance to my sheaf" (Gen. 37:7). His brothers, assaulting him with malicious questions, "hated him yet the more" (Gen. 37:8).

And he dreamed yet another dream, and told it his brethren, and said, Behold, I have dreamed a dream more; and, behold, the sun and the moon and the eleven stars made obeisance to me. And he told it to his father, and to his brethren: and his father rebuked him, and said unto him, What is this dream that thou hast dreamed? Shall I and thy mother and thy brethren indeed come to bow down ourselves to thee to the earth? (Gen. 37:9-10).

When I was a boy, I dreamed a dream which was with me when I slept and when I was awake. I used to plow and look up at some of the white thunderheads in the sky and say to myself that sometime in the years ahead I would be pastor of a big and great church in a big city—that I would no longer troop between the plow handles behind a stubborn white mule the heels of which were wicked.

Did my dream come true? Yes. Yes. I say this with no boast in my heart or mouth.

My desire to be pastor of a big church in a big city was not a babbling brook bit but a surging river in my ambition.

My ambition to be—in the future years—pastor of a big church with many members in a big city with its multitudes was not a little sapling but a tall redwood tree in the forest of my thinking. My purpose all along was as a fire that would not die down—a fire that needed no extra wood on the hearthstone.

AND here comes some of the Bellevue story:

I was pastor 1925-1927 of the Citadel Square Baptist Church. We averaged over one thousand per Sunday during my stay there. Fine and faithful, giving me fellowship for my leadership, was the membership. There, after a revival meeting in which I did the preaching, I baptized eighty-three in one night. There my little daughter made her confession of faith, and I baptized her one Sunday afternoon in the lake in the park.

There was no reason why I could not have stayed at Citadel Square for years. But one Saturday afternoon, I went to my office and I saw a man in the auditorium, walking around and looking around. I greeted him. He said: "I am J. E. Dilworth, chairman of the pulpit committee of Bellevue Baptist Church, and I came this long distance by train from Memphis to Charleston to talk to you about becoming the Bellevue pastor."

In my office that same afternoon, he showed me what he called advantages of Bellevue over Citadel Square, and of Memphis over Charleston.

He showed me a map and said: "Look! there is nothing on the east of Charleston but the Atlantic Ocean, and there is no prospect of Charleston growing in population as will Memphis. He put his finger on the map. "Look!" he said, "North, East, West, and South of Memphis there are and will be multitudes of people—and you will have the chance to lead us in having one of the greatest churches in the land. You lead. And we will follow."

I was greatly impressed. And sadness, too, laid hold on my heart as I thought again of saying good-bye to a people I loved—even as I had said good-bye in New Orleans. I gave Mr. Dilworth no assurance that I wanted to move from Charleston to Memphis.

"We want you," he said.

He went back to Memphis. I got a message from the church that they wanted me for pastor.

I wrote the pulpit committee that I had an engagement at the First Baptist Church, Shreveport, Louisiana, on a certain Sunday, and that I would stop by Memphis on my way to Shreveport and talk with the pulpit committee and "look things over." I did. They showed me over the church building and their "holdings"—an auditorium half as large as Citadel Square and they told me the Sunday School "ran around five hundred."

After I returned from Shreveport to Charleston, by train all those weary miles, I wrote the chairman, Mr. Dilworth, that I could not feel led to accept their offer to become pastor of Bellevue.

Three weeks after that I had a change of mind and heart. One morning I said to Mrs. Myrtis Watson, my secretary, "I have made a mistake."

She asked: "What sort of mistake?"

"I ought to have accepted the Bellevue offer. Send a wire to Mr. Dilworth and tell him I am willing and ready to come to Bellevue and Memphis, IF they still want me."

"But suppose they have called someone"? she asked.

"No." I said, "the way I feel in my heart I know they could not have called anyone."

She sent the wire.

In forty-five minutes, I had the reply. The pulpit committee would meet me in Atlanta at the Piedmont Hotel and "talk matters over with me and have an understanding about everything."

We met on the day and at the hour agreed upon. They put the opportunities and responsibilities of Bellevue heavily on my heart, with an earnestness seldom shown by pulpit committees. They went back to Memphis.

Then Bellevue called me. Before the call was extended, some members, hearing that the church was "getting ready to call" sent some telegrams to certain men in South Carolina asking "what sort of a man and preacher is Dr. Lee?" They seemed to distrust the evaluation of the pulpit committee and wanted to hear me preach before they voted on the committee's recommendation. They were informed that I did not believe in "trial sermons" and would not preach one. I have said that any fool can shoot one big gun!

Anyway, Bellevue called me. I accepted—under criticism from some. "Did you hear Lee is going to Memphis?" A Baptist minister directed this question to one of his colleagues, who replied: "No, I haven't heard, but he won't stay long. Lee is a 'mover.' He never stays long in any one place."

Just before I began my ministry at Bellevue, I preached in an eight-day revival effort at the First Baptist Church of Birmingham, Alabama.

My wife and two children took the train from Greenville, South Carolina, where they got to spend a week with my wife's mother. I got on the train with them at Birmingham and we arrived in Memphis the morning of December 10.

We were taken to the home of J. E. Dilworth. He then carried us to a home the church had rented for the preacher and his family until we could buy a house. The church had no parsonage. After one month on Autumn Avenue, I bought a house for seven thousand dollars on Peach Avenue—paying down one hundred dollars and signing notes for one hundred a month and interest. We lived in this little bungalow for forty-one years!

Bellevue! During my ministry, there were sad days and glad days, bad days and good days, little days and death days. And wedding days, tragic days and triumphant days. But EVERY DAY WAS A PAY DAY FROM GOD!

I preached my first sermon to a congregation that had never seen me, though a few might have heard me preach somewhere. I told them my motto for them was 2 Corinthians 12:15: "And I will very gladly spend and be spent for you; though the more abundantly I love you, the less I be loved."

My text for my first sermon was Judges 20:11: "The men of Israel were gathered against the city, knit together as one man." I told the folks that together the bricks make the wall; together the links make the chain; together the trees make the forest; together the soldiers make the army; together the cents make the dollars. And that if we would love and work and pray together great things could be done.

Though at first the Sunday School was about half as large as the Sunday School at Citadel Square in Charleston, there was a great increase in Sunday School attendance and church membership. I baptized converts every Sunday night.

At first the B.Y.P.U. attendance was sixty-two—quite a difference in that and the later time when the B.Y.P.U. was called the Training Union, and we had a world-record attendance one Sunday night of 2656. The membership of Bellevue Baptist Church in 1927 was 1430, and 254 of these could not be found.

I gave the people leadership as I believed I got it from God, and they gave me "fellowship." I used to say about my Bellevue people: "I have to be careful what I ask them to do. If I ask them to jump in the river, I'll hear water splash. If I ask them to walk in the fire, I'll smell clothes burning."

God was leading and blessing at Bellevue. But the great financial crash that came in October, 1929, put a strain upon the faith and pocketbooks of the people. But the church had to have some Sunday School buildings—since the fire department of Memphis had condemned the frail building used for Sunday School purposes. I led the people to enlarge the church auditorium and to build some Sunday School buildings—at a cost not to exceed $225,000. On June 30, 1930, ground was broken for the new buildings and the enlargement of the worship auditorium.

Great joy was in the hearts of all November 23, 1930, the day when the enlarged auditorium was filled to overflowing. Forty-seven people united with the church that Sunday. Soon after entering the enlarged auditorium, the new education building was ready for use.

The financial stress was felt terribly severely in 1930, and many criticized me for "leading the church into debt." One banker said to me: "You are a good man, but you're sunk. You'll never get your members to pay the debt and other expenses of the church, too!"

I said to him: "You talk like God was dead."

Some said: "The preacher will do what he did in New Orleans—get the church in debt and leave." And others made such remarks as, "Bellevue is on the downgrade." "You can't pay that much interest"; "The bonds will be no good"; and "Folks will not join a church that is in debt." One man, leaving the membership of the church, said: "I'm not going to be there when the crash comes."

I preached to my people a sermon on "The Contagion of Faintheartedness" from the text Deuteronomy 20:8: "What man is there that is fearful and fainthearted? let him go and return unto his house, lest his brethren's heart faint as well as his heart." I kept telling the people that, as Dr. F. B. Meyer said, we never test the resources of God until we attempt the impossible.

In these trying times, some seemed to forget that my first year at Bellevue 148 people had been recieved into the church by confession of faith and 452 persons had united with the church by letter from other churches, a total of six hundred members in one year.

The financial depression was depressing indeed. The crash of the stock market was resounding. Brokers sold stock for any price they could get. In a half a day, eight million shares had changed hands. By mid-November of the first depression year the stocks listed on the New York Exchange had fallen over forty percent in value—a loss on paper that exceeded twenty-five billion dollars.

In Memphis tenants were asking credit of landlords. The corner grocer passed out his bread, groceries, and vegetables on credit. Many store owners lost their business. To get cash, jewelry—even wedding rings—were pawned. Some sold their furniture. By the spring of 1930, there were over one million Americans unemployed. In large cities bread lines were nearly a mile long. In Memphis, on many street corners, men who had been well fixed in business were selling apples.

For the first time since the Jackson Era a President of the United States was openly booed. Cries of "Down with Hoover" could be heard in many places. People in their conversation referred to "Hell, Hoover, and Hard Times." Hoover knew despondency, and despair paralyzed him.

Quivers full of critical arrows were shot at me. Here are some other remarks I heard:

"We can't pay that much interest."

"The bonds will be no good."

"Where is the money coming from?"

"This is the end."

"Lee ought to preach the gospel and not try to build buildings."

Because of my insistence on the need for buildings, I was accused of not believing in missions. A Baptist editor advised certain members of Bellevue that they ought to move their membership to another church, because, "Dr. Lee does not believe in missions." No statement could have been further from the truth, and when I heard about it, I said: "If I don't believe in missions, the sun is an iceberg, and Jenny Lind has a beard."

Two of my men came to me and asked that I lead the way in seeing to it that the church give no more to missions until the staggering debt was lessened.

I told them I could not agree to do such a thing. They began to argue, talking about "what a mess the church was in financially." I said: "Brethren, please don't argue with me. You are barking up a tree where there is no 'possum."

They left despondent, and their despondency was increased when the church had to sell second mortgage bonds to the amount of $47,000, with 7 percent interest to get enough money to finish construction of the buildings, we were under contract to build.

I went off for a week for a revival meeting in Jackson, Mississippi. There I received a telegram from Frank D. Fuller, chariman of the building committee, stating: "Absolutely necessary that you be here tomorrow to attending meeting of the building committee—otherwise the whole program is lost. Sorry to interfere with your meeting, but your presence alone can save situation. You can leave on midnight train."

I came home for a day, and pumped up the flat tires of members of the building committee. And they began again to move in faith.

The finances of the Bellevue Baptist Church presented a grievous problem for three years. These were times when money had to be borrowed from banks to pay interest on the first and second mortgage bonds. Reading the minutes, you will see that the finance committee stood with me to carry the church through these difficult times, trusting in God.

Excerpts from the minutes will reveal the serious problem that the finances presented at this time:

May 11, 1930: Borrow $10,000 temporarily in order to take up and retire the present outstanding bonds.

October 21, 1931: The meeting called for the purpose of borrowing up to $4,500. for retirement of $10,000, second mortgage bonds on November 1.

June 23, 1932: Special meeting of the Board of Deacons called for the purpose of borrowing $7,500.

November 23, 1932: Mr. J. E. Dilworth made a motion, which was seconded by Mr. E. F. Green, that the finance committee be authorized to borrow $2,000 to pay current obligations subject to the approval of the church.

December 21, 1932: Mr. Fuller made motion which was seconded by E. F. Green, that the Board go before the church and request authority to borrow approximately $6,000 to pay interest on first mortgage bonds due January 1st.

At this time, I demanded that my salary be reduced from $7,000 a year to $6,000, even though I was paying for a home and furnishing my own car.

The financial crisis continued but the work at Bellevue flourished. This paradox was constantly reflected in 1932. In May there were 104 additions, 46 of whom were accepted as candidates for baptism.

On May 31, 1932, there were over two thousand persons in Sunday School. But although the membership of Bellevue had doubled in three years, the total money receipts were twenty thousand less than they had been in 1929. Yes! But soon the financial growth of the church matched the numerical growth. And in 1956, the money receipts were $723,793.

AND now—what more shall I say? An effort to mention and portray all the achievements at Bellevue is like a masked diver diving deep into pearl beds and coming up with both hands full of pearls but leaving more pearls behind than he brings up.

But mention must be made of one great day in Bellevue's life. One Sunday morning, some hours before church service time, three Bellevue members brought to my office a young mother and her three children—all under nine years of age. All of them were hungry. The children began to cry. The mother struggled to keep back the sobs and tears.

Then she told me how her husband had gone to work on Friday morning, but disappeared later that day. None of the men with whom he worked could tell where he had gone, but he had left the shop at 4 P.M. The mother said that the children had had nothing to eat since early Saturday morning, and the mother had no money to buy food. I told them to quit crying, gave them enough money to have food for two days. The mother sobbed out her thanks.

I prayed for all of them. As I prayed, a hush came, and the children were happy at the prospect of being fed. I said: "Now, I want all of you grown folks to pray for me. This little mother is a Christian and she can pray. I want you to pray for our church services today that God will give us a good day. I am to hold our yearly March evangelistic service in the Junior Department. Then I am going to preach in the morning service. Then we are to observe the Lord's Supper. I am to have Mr. Shangle's funeral this afternoon at three. I am to preach tonight. So pray that God will give me strength sufficient for the tasks of the day. Then I want all of you to pray for me, because tomorrow I leave for Korea to preach for three weeks at the Korean Baptist Convention and at one of the seminaries and to the soldiers in the Korean army and hold a revival meeting in Pusan. Pray that I will get back safely from the long flight across the oceans and over the mountains."

It seemed as though someone had wrapped a warm blanket about me. There was a sensation as though someone's tender fingertips were caressing me, up and down my body—it seemed as if warm and soft lips were pressed repeatedly against my cheeks. I was warm all over, from the top of my head to the bottom of my feet.

Never in all my life did I have such a strange and mysterious feeling.

The experience, unbelievable to me, was unforgettable to me.

Someone spoke to me—God, I believe—saying: "There is going to be a great day at Bellevue today, and then something hurtful is going to happen to you."

As I quit praying, I was deeply conscious of the warmth, the caressing, and the strange voice that brought a message of both good and bad.

As the group turned to go, I said to them: "Wait a minute, I want to tell you something. We are going to have a great day in the church today, and then something is going to happen to me."

"Oh, Dr. Lee," exclaimed one of the group, "what do you mean?" "Just that," I replied, "Just that! God has made it known to me. But I must get ready for the service in the Junior Department."

After this, the day went into full swing, and about nine-thirty, I went to the Junior Department of the Sunday School—a department made up of about three hundred youngsters in the age bracket of nine to twelve years. There I made use of the Bible, explaining passages of Scripture which set forth the essentials of how a person can become a Christian. The presentation made plain the plan of salvation. Then I gave a simple invitation for the children who were willing to put their trust in Jesus to come forward and make a public profession of such faith. There were about twenty boys and girls who came forward to make a decision for Christ.

As I left the Junior Department, one of the teachers, a deacon, said: "Preacher, I have been teaching in this department for twenty years, and I never saw you as you looked this morning. You were never so effective in your speaking, and these youngsters were never so attentive. There seemed to be something unusual in it all."

"Yes," I said, "It was a good service, and I am so glad. But I must go now and get on my white suit for the preaching hour and be on time."

That morning, I preached a brief sermon—something I have seldom done through the years. I selected for my text the words "And he brought him to Jesus" (John 1:42). I spoke simply and earnestly and with a quiet intensity, and pictured that New Testament scene which tells what happened to John and Andrew after they had been in the presence of Jesus. Each of the disciples became engrossed with the same idea—to go and tell his brother about having seen Christ. Andrew "First findeth his own brother Simon, and saith unto him, we have found the Messias, which is, being interpreted, the Christ. And he brought him to Jesus" (John 1:41-42).

I pointed out that one of the greatest things any person can do in this life is "to bring another to Jesus." I urged people to believe that for a Christian to win another to faith in Christ is a greater work than to write a best seller, than to lead an army to victory, than to win a presidential election—yes, the greatest work that ever moved an angel's wing in flight, that ever moved God's heart in compassion, that ever laid claim upon Christian's faith and education and abilities.

I declared that a man coming to Christ finds forgiveness of all sins, solace for life's many sorrows, prompting for life's perplexities, help in life's hazards, direction in life's doubts. All that and more does it mean to be brought out of one's "bondage, sorrow, and night" into Christ's "freedom, gladness and light." I then laid upon the minds of that Sunday morning congregation the importance of giving consideration to coming to Jesus.

I gave the invitation. People seemed to forget themselves, their circumstances, their problems, as they came forward. I felt again the same warm sensation which I felt earlier in my office.

I made an appeal to the lost to accept Christ and for those who were Baptists without a church home in Memphis to come and join the Bellevue membership.

Also an appeal was made for those who were already Christians to come and renew their loyalty to Christ. I addressed my words to those who were giving God a tame half-heartedness, and to the Christians who were do-little and do-nothing Christians to make their lives count more for Christ.

The people began to respond. There was a march down the aisle to the front. Children came, young people came, older people came. The whole congregation was as a forest stirred by an invisible wind.

Many handkerchiefs were used to dry weeping eyes.

A prominent lawyer came forward, sobbingly confessing his wrong-doing, and saying: "Preacher, I thank God for you and what you said today, and for what you have done for me. I've been hating somebody in this church for ten years. Not a day of these ten years but I have hated him. But I am going to him this afternoon and ask his forgiveness and tell him I am going to love him and I want him to love me."

While I was in Korea, this lawyer had a fatal seizure while addressing a jury in the court room.

A young woman came forward. She was lavishly dressed with jewelry on her ears and around her neck, and her fingers sparkled with diamonds. The young lady came and cried loud enough for all in the sanctuary to hear: "Oh, sir, I have never made my life count for anything for God, but I am going to from now on, I am! I am! God help me."

There was a handsome young man who came and in anguish cried: "I would have died if I had stayed back there. I would have died. I had to come, sir, I had to."

The whole congregation was visibly moved, there were tears everywhere, and bowed head, and silent prayers were being spoken. The invitation continued and the people sang, though some of the choir, overcome by the power of the Holy Spirit moving their hearts, could sing only chokingly.

The invitation continued—it was past noon—and the people kept coming. The hands of the clock swept past twelve-thirty and approached one o'clock. The invitation lasted one hour. Standing at the front and around the walls were 126 persons. Many of these came upon confession of faith asking for baptism, many came on promise of a church letter. Many came promising God to make their lives more meaningful.

W. C. Graves, son of the great preacher, J. R. Graves, and a deacon for years, made this statement to me after the service: "I have been going to church since I was six years of age, and I have been going through many worship services when I was young and now that I am old. I must say I have never seen any congregation so moved and I have never felt anything like this we have had today. None of us have seen it in this wise. Bridges have been built across gulfs today. Burdens have been lifted and joy increased, mine too, souls saved! We were made to forget everything today but Jesus."

I stopped the invitation at a quarter till one. I took the hand and spoke a few words to each and all of the 126 who had come forward, a long line of people.

Then I said this to the congregation: "We were to have the observance of the Lord's Supper this morning. But this glorious hour is a late hour by the clock, and this afternoon, right here in this building we have Mr. Shangle's funeral and many of you will want to be present. We shall observe the Lord's Supper tonight."

That afternoon, I conducted the funeral of Mr. C. B. Shangle. At the night service, there was another good response to the invitation. That night I baptized fifty-three people. Standing in the baptistry, I said to the people: "We were to observe the Lord's Supper tonight since we could not do so this morning. The hour is very late, and I am asking you to decide if we shall take time for the observance tonight." The people voted to go ahead with the observance, and the Supper was observed with joy and gratitude and reverence.

I said that night, even as I have said many times since: "I think that since the Day of Pentecost God has never given a church a greater day than we have experienced this day at Bellevue. Nobody can go through a day like this and doubt the reality of the Holy Spirit and his work in convicting people of sin, of righteousness, and of judgment. The tree from which such fruit fell today was a tree shaken by the Holy Spirit. The movement among people today was as when, in Ezekiel's day, the valley of dry bones became a living army."

At bedtime that night I was physically exhausted, but there was peace and elation in my heart. I went to sleep wondering just what would be the "something" that would happen to me.

On Monday morning, March 26, I packed for my long trip in Korea, and attended the men's prayer meeting held in the church dining room. All of the men took turns praying that their pastor would be afforded traveling mercies, that he would be mightily used of God, and that he return to them safely. Later Mrs. Lee drove me to the airport, but not until she had taken me to the Shangle home for a time of prayer with the woman whose husband I had buried the day before.

At the airport was a host of people to see me and one of my young deacons, Mr. Hugh Dyer, off. As we two boarded the plane, the friends joined in singing, "God will take care of you."

Strapped to my seat, ready for the take-off, I said to Dyer: "I am lifeless. Hope I'm not going to be sick." The deacon said, "You will be fine when you are rested and get some sleep."

When the plane reached Seattle, Dyer and I were rerouted through Anchorage, Alaska, where at midnight, we waited for two hours while some mechanical adjustments were made on the plane's motors. After midnight, with sleet pelting down and the cold wind blowing, the plane took off for Japan. Enroute, the plane landed at Cold Harbor, where amid falling snow and icy winds, all passengers were taken off, put in an open truck, and driven three miles to a small hut where they found a red-hot, pot-bellied stove warming the room. We were grateful for the warmth. After about two hours, an open truck came and took us back to the plane. I was cold and shivering. Never in my life could I remember feeling worse unless it was the experience when I had the black water fever in Panama at twenty-one years of age.

When the passengers had gotten settled in their seats, the pilot came back from his cabin and apologetically told them that the machine for melting ice on the plane's wings was still out of order, and that they could not stand the cold in the plane and would have to return to the hut for comfort.

Out of the plane and into an open truck and back to the hut with the pot-bellied stove, the passengers went. It was zero weather. I did not know whether I could survive the ordeal. There after two hours of comfort in the hut, the open truck arrived, and through the biting cold the passengers were taken back to the plane. There followed a nineteen-hour flight to Tokyo.

I recalled the words, "And then something hurtful is going to happen to you." Dyer buttoned up my overcoat and wrapped two blankets around me. I shivered, my teeth chattered, I was miserable. I felt as though a sheet of ice, not a blanket, was around my back. Weakly I said, "Hugh, I am sick, and I don't mean halfway sick, but completely sick, and without energy." My condition was more desperate because there was neither a doctor nor a nurse on the plane to provide medical attention.

Twelve missionaries greeted Dyer and me when we arrived in Tokyo. The time required to go through customs seemed interminable. I had no strength but strove to hide my weakness. I was so cold during the supper period that I kept on my overcoat—a small gas stove was nearby to lessen the coldness.

After supper, we were taken to the living room of the mission home, where at the request of the missionaries, I was asked to talk. I could hardly think, much less talk. Finally I surrendered all effort to put on a brave front, and explained that I was sick and needed to go to bed. I did go to bed and experienced a troubled night, suffering from weakness, chills, and passing of blood.

Some Japanese pastors came to visit me in the morning. Through a missionary interpreter, I tried to talk with them, but my voice was so weak that almost all I said was unintelligible. I did succeed in conveying the need for a doctor, and Dr. Eitel, who used to be with the China Inland Mission and now had a clinic in Tokyo, was summoned. As he came into the room, he exclaimed: "Well, whom do we have here? And what's the matter with him?" He put his stethoscope on my chest and listened. Then, he said: "Here, here, get this man to a hospital *right now,* and I don't mean ten minutes from now. I mean *now!*"

I was bundled up in pajamas, an overcoat, and a blanket and really rushed to the old Saibo Hospital. As we went up on the elevator, it seemed I could hardly stand—and I was chilled. The little Japanese nurses looked to me like snow men. I was put in the hospital for fifteen days.

One night I thought I was dying. I called for Hugh Dyer. He had gone somewhere to spend the night at the request of some missionary. I wanted to give my wife and my Bellevue people a message—a last message—from me. The little Japanese nurses ran to my bedside in answer to my "buzzer." They got excited. They got in touch with Dr. Eitel. He came and stayed until dawn with me, ministering to me and praying for me.

Ere he came, I had an argument with God. I told him I did not want to die and that if he would make me well and take me home alive instead of in a Japanese coffin, I would do my best to do my best preaching. I was reverent but as earnest as Hezekiah who turned his face to the wall and prayed and asked God to grant him other days.

Dr. Eitel said that I with my blood pressure down to sixty-five sat on the edge of the grave with my legs hanging into it. But God heard my prayer, just as he heard the prayer of Hezekiah (Isa. 38:1-5). That night when I thought the hour of death had come, I "placed all the faculties of heart and body at the feet of the Saviour." The voice which said, "Something hurtful is going to happen to you" had spoken the truth.

Although all 38 speaking engagements scheduled for me in Korea had to be cancelled, I presented the gospel on five occasions to the Koreans. As a result about sixty people indicated acceptance of Christ in the Baptist Church in Seoul where no heat warmed the cold auditorium.

While I was in Seoul, Dr. Louise Yim, who was president of Chungang University, a school of five thousand Koreans, invited me to her home. This gracious and great woman at luncheon served in her stone home which was nearly five hundred years old, said: "Dr. Lee, I know you have not been well since you came to this side of the world, but you must not go back to America without speaking to my students in my university. God will give you strength for it. So you must speak to them."

I accepted the invitation, and the next day—in the afternoon of a day of sunshine—we went to the University. Dr. Yim personally escorted me to the campus and through many buildings and classrooms. Then, out on the campus where a platform had been built and a loudspeaker set up, I spoke to more than two thousand students who stood and listened earnestly. I spoke of "Jesus"—employing his preexistence, virgin birth, sinless life, sacrificial cross, and triumphant resurrection.

Dr. Yim, a fluent speaker of the English language, a graduate of an American University, translated my message. At the close of my sermon of about twenty-five minutes in length, I said this: "Now, all of you who believe what I have said about Jesus and are willing to accept him as Savior and trust him for all matters of life in which you need help, hold up your hand." More than a hundred students held up their hands—the fingers clenched into a fist formation—signifying determination.

Dr. John A. Abernathy, Southern Baptist missionary in Seoul, Korea, wrote me these words about the service:

We often think of your visit to Korea. And although you were unwell, how refreshing it was for us and to our dear Korean people. You preached at Central University that morning to the thousands of students. I remember around one hundred fine students confessed Christ as Saviour and Lord at the close. John A. Abernathy

Once again back at Bellevue, an overwhelming sense of gratitude swept over me. I had undergone a close brush with death. There were moments when I thought I would never see my wife again, moments when I felt I would never again stand in my Bellevue pulpit and preach again. Now that God had spared me I was determined to keep the promise I made to God if he would spare my life.

8

Chuckles Along the Line

Floor License

Jerry Moore was, physically, a thin, skinny, yet muscular, black man with bright eyes. His tongue and mouth sputtered out words about as fast as a machine gun spits out bullets.

Jerry was a bachelor of twenty-five who said he wanted no wife "because dese women are so uncertain."

Jerry was a faithful church member and was pleased if his pastor called on him to pray. Some said he spoke so rapidly only God could "keep up with him."

This handy man often worked around our house and garden in Waterloo—a little town of two hundred population. He showed up for work just as Mrs. Lee was cooking breakfast and quit the day's work when the smell of fried country ham came from our kitchen door.

One day this handy man—a sort of lay preacher—came to me with his usual greeting which was, "Yes, suh, Doc, yes, suh!" Then he said, "I done got a flo (floor) license at our church."

"What do you mean, Jerry, about a flo (floor) license?" I asked.

"De pastor and deacons won't let me speak from up on the pulpit behind the Bible stand but they let me speak from down on de flo (floor) in front of the Bible stand," he said rapidly.

Later after this declaration about his flo (floor) license, Jerry came to me.

"Yes, suh, Doc, yes, suh", he said, "We gointer have a fifth Saddy and Sunday meeting out at our church, and I am going to exercise my flo (floor) license. An' I wants you to give me some of your sermon notes and a printed-out sermon, please, suh."

I gave Jerry a few of my sermon outline notes and a printed-out sermon.

He came to the back door of our house Monday morning, following the fifth Sunday meeting. My wife was frying bacon and eggs. I went to the door.

"Good morning, Jerry," I said.

"Yes, suh, Doc, Yes, suh! Good mornin'," he answered.

"Did you go to the fifth Saturday and Sunday meeting, Jerry?"

"Yes, suh, Doc—and everybody there, too—everybody!"

"Did you use my sermon notes and printed-out sermon?" I asked.

"Yes, suh, Doc, sho did, sho did!" he said.

"How did you get along with them?" I asked.

"Jes fine, suh! *And I improve 'em greatly.* Yes, suh, yes, suh!"

I Hold 'em on My Knife

Dr. Ellis A. Fuller, once pastor of the First Baptist Church, Atlanta, Georgia, and once president of the Southern Baptist Theological Seminary, was a dear friend of mine. Our lives were something like the David-Jonathan relationship.

I was once his pastor and the pastor of his parents and his brother and sister in our early ministry. Dr. Fuller, at first, was not much in favor of the radio Baptist Hour when it was first put before the Southern Baptist Convention.

He said: "I believe money given to the Seminary may do more good than money thrown into the air by radio."

I had fought hard along with the noble Sam Lowe for the Southern Baptist Convention to have the Baptist Hour via radio.

I wrote Fuller these words: "Beloved Ellis, as to the Baptist Hour, you are eating with your knife. Love, Bob."

He wrote back: "Beloved Bob:

"With my peas I always eat honey,

I've done so all my life;

It makes the peas taste funny,

But it holds 'em on my knife—Love, Ellis"

A Preacher's Voice But . . .

Dr. A. J. Barton—great in all ways and in all places—was a dear friend of mine. Once he went to Washington to have a meeting with the President of the United States.

He went to a barber shop in the capitol building. The black barber said: "Boss, dis am the Congressional bank shop."

Dr. Barton asked: "Well, you shave senators, don't you?"

"Yes, sir, yes, sir, take the chair, sir!"

Dr. Barton sat in the chair. The barber turned the chair so that Dr. Barton was in a horizontal position. Then the barber got suspicious. He began to lather Dr. Barton's face. Then he asked: "Boss, what is you?"

"Dr. Barton asked: "Well, what do think I am?"

The barber said: "I don't know, suh! You have a preacher's voice, but you have a mighty ungodly face!"

Enough of War

A black soldier was returning home, after being scarred and wounded on the battlefields in France. As the ship on which he voyaged entered New York harbor, the soldier took off his cap in a gesture of respect as he looked at the Statue of Liberty. Then he said aloud: "Here I is, Ole Lady, if you ever sees me again, you gwanter have to turn around."

Bad Definition

Once when I was principal of a public school, I had a football team which I coached as best I could. Jim Riley was a tousled-headed, muscular, speedy boy I often played at the quarterback position. Jim liked football but had little liking for study. One day I lectured half-an-hour in the physiology class, telling of the functions of different members of the human body. After the lecture, I wrote a five-question quiz on the blackboard in the classroom. One question was: "Locate and describe the alimentary canal."

Jim wrote me out this answer, which I have in his own hand scribbling today in one of my old scrapbooks: "The alimentary canal is located between the Mediterranean Sea and the Red Sea. It is forty miles long and is owned by Great Britian."

I suppose I should have flunked him, but there was a game coming up between our school and our chief rival in the football area, and I needed Jim to be the quarterback.

Subject and Text

In the Lauren County Baptist Association it was the custom to have fifth Saturday and fifth Sunday meetings, with preaching in the morning and afternoon and "dinner on the church grounds."

Brother Caleb Lancaster, a sweet and noble old man of seventy years, always conducted what he called the devotional at ten A.M. each fifth Saturday. The program committee never put anybody except Brother Caleb on for the ten A.M. hour.

Brother Caleb Lancaster would go to the pulpit stand, open the Bible, pull his octagon-shaped glasses far down on his nose, look out at the congregation over his glasses, and say: "Well, dear folks, what verse my eye lights on I talks on."

One morning, his eye "lit upon" Isaiah, the eighth chapter. In the first verse were these words: "Moreover the Lord said unto me, Take thee a great roll, and write in it with a man's pen concerning Mahershalalhashbaz" (Isa. 8:1).

Brother Lancaster let his eyes "light" several times upon the verse. Then he said, with a bit of confusion, "I ain't never met that brother, and I ain't gointer speak to him today."

At another time, at the fifth Saturday morning meeting, his eyes "lit" upon 2 Samuel 21:20: "And there was yet a battle in Gath, where was a man of great stature, that had on every hand six fingers, and on every foot six toes, four and twenty in number; and he also was born to the giant."

His comments upon that verse were something like this: "That shorely was a big guy! And if he had five-finger gloves, they wouldn't help. And if he had ingrowing toenails, he must have suffered a lot. My wife suffered for days when she had just one ingrowing toenail."

While we were eating "dinner on the grounds" at the tables loaded with all sorts of foods, I said to this great old man: "Brother Lancaster, I am just a young sprout and you are a giant tree in God's forest, and maybe I should not say to you what I am going to say. But why don't you get you a subject and a text, and you could say some good things that would help folks. So, please, sir, quit getting up and saying that "the first verse your eye lights on you talks on."

Three months later the fifth Saturday and Sunday meeting was held at the grand old Prospect Baptist Church. Brother Lancaster took his place before the Bible stand in the pulpit. He pulled his octagon spectacles far down on his nose, and said: "Well, dear folks! The last time I had this devotional, Brother Lee over here (and he nodded his head toward me), said I ought to quit getting up and telling you that the first verse my eye lights on, I talks on. So I got me a subject and a text. My subject is "Christian Activity" and you can find my text in the first verse of chapter number five of Second Kings—"Naaman was a leper." He pronounced "leper" as though it was "leaper." And he proceeded to tell us that Naaman did not sit down when there was something to be done, but he LEAPED. He did not stroll around, but LEAPED. He did not walk slowly or just run, but he LEAPED. And he urged us to believe that the churches needed "a mighty host of LEAPERS," not crawlers, not sitters, not strollers, not lame walkers—but LEAPERS.

Dislike for Sermon

One Sunday morning years ago, I "took off" against liquor and liquor drinking. I made it plain that I believe that hell-deserving were those who made liquor, those who sold liquor, and those who drank the hellish stuff. I quoted Abraham Lincoln who said that liquor has defenders but no defense. I, quoting another, said that the best way to get along with liquor is to get along without it.

I believe that liquor never touched an individual, that it did not leave an indelible stain, never touched a home it did not plant the seeds of dissolution and misery, never touched a community that it did not lower the moral tone, never was legalized by a government that it did not increase that government's problems, lessen patriotism, and increase treason.

I said that booze was bad—as bad as poison ivy and sewerage in a drinking fountain, as bad as strychnine in a baby's milk bottle, as bad as poison ivy in a bride's bouquet, as bad as a mad dog on a children's playground, as bad as a rattlesnake in a kindergarten, as bad as a rapist in a girl's dormitory, as bad as a maniac wielding a razor in an old folks home.

I declared vehemently that only a fool would make it, only a fool would sell it, only a fool would buy it and drink it.

At the close of the service, a man came by and stuck out his hand. To shake his hand was like stroking an icicle. A frown covered all his face. His voice was half a snarl when he said, "I didn't like your sermon."

I said: "The devil didn't either. Classify yourself and come back next Sunday."

Chopping with a Dull Ax

In 1910, I was pastor of the Fairview Baptist Church—a country church near Greer, South Carolina. I was pastor of a great and noble country preacher named Ben Vaughan. His kindness and helpfulness to me I shall never forget. One Sunday morning in my preaching, I was like a bird with a broken wing—I never got off the ground. I knew I had done poorly.

Brother Ben took me home with him for dinner. As we walked to his house—not so far from the church—he said with a sort of hesitancy: "Brother Lee, before you come back for your next Sunday with us, I want you to search the Scriptures. You know it is good for *all* preachers and especially *young* preachers to search the scriptures. Somewhere in the book of Ecclesiastes, you will find, if you search for it, a verse I want you to learn and put into practice when you come back. The verse says something about a dull ax."

The verse was: "If the iron be blunt, and he do not whet the edge, then must he put to more strength: but wisdom is profitable to direct" (Eccl. 10:10).

When I went back to preach again, I used as a text these words: "And Benaiah the son of Jehoiada, the son of a valiant man, of Kabzeel, who had done so many acts, he slew two lionlike men of Moab: he went down also and slew a lion in the midst of a pit in time of snow" (2 Sam. 23:20).

Again I ate dinner after the preaching hour. As we ate dinner, Brother Ben said to all the folks at the table, "Our pastor didn't chop with a dull ax today."

I have tried not to "chop with a dull ax" ever since.

A Chicken Coop

One hot Sunday in the First Baptist Church in New Orleans I doubtless tried to chop wood with just an ax handle with no ax.

Anyway, I got down a dead-end street and could not turn around. I came up against a thick briar hedge and could not go through. I missed the nail and hit my finger several times with my preaching hammer. I was so conscious of failure until I stopped half-way in my message. I gave the invitation, and the four people who joined the church did not lessen the woe of my conscious inadequacy.

The chairman of the deacons—Brother J. H. Tharpe—came to me and said: "Preacher, would you like to go riding?" I said: "I surely would."

He asked: "How far would you like to go?

I answered: "You could not take me as far as I would like to go."

He got me in his car and drove a long way up St. Charles Avenue. He had driven at least three miles before a word was said.

Then turning to him with some embarrassment, I asked: "Beloved, what *was* the matter with me this morning?"

He drove on to Sophie Newcombe College—two miles further—before he answered. Then with frankness he said: "Beloved, you laid a skyscraper foundation and built a chicken coop on it."

Could Not Spell

Some years ago, twenty college students were riding a bus to Ridgecrest, North Carolina. On the side of the bus were fastened a few college banners. Then alone in big-size, the letters *B.S.U.*

The bus stopped at a mountain gasoline station to "fill up with gas." A little mountain boy, curiously interested, stood and looked at the bus.

Then he asked: "Are you folks college folks?"

When assured that they were, he answered with rebuking soberness: "Wa'al, you ain't got much education—'cause you can't spell BUS!"

Here Lies a Foolish Swine

Sometimes when I address civic clubs, I begin my message by saying: "I hope you will get more out of my message than a Memphis man got out of the Rock Island Railroad. This man owned a hog farm

in Arkansas. One day a train ran over one of his razor-back hogs
and killed it. The man wrote the railroad authorities this verse:

> My razorback
> Strolled down your track
> A week ago today.
> Your twenty nine came down the line
> And snuffed his life away.
> You can't blame me—
> The hog you see
> Strolled through a cattle gate
> So kindly pen
> A check for ten,
> That debt to liquidate.

A clerk in the railroad main office answered with these words:

> Our Twenty Nine
> Came down the line
> And killed your hog, we know,
> But razorbacks
> On railroad tracks
> Quite often meet with woe
> Therefore, my friend,
> We cannot send
> The check for which you pine.
> Just bury the dead—
> Write over his head:
> "Here lies a foolish swine."

9.
Some Folks I Have Met

It has been a case of Payday Everyday, considering the people with whom I have shaken hands and with whom I have spoken, and whose voices I have heard. I mention a few.

DR. W. B. RILEY

Pastor, First Baptist Church, Minneapolis, Minnesota, for about half a century. Founder of a great educational institution. Handsome man he. And wonderfully attractive and effective in speaking.

He said: "The preaching, the teaching, the theology that does not make sin stink is puny preaching, trite teaching, and tragic theology."

DR. J. H. JOWETT

Mighty Presbyterian preacher—a superb master and user of the English language. I was only nineteen when I met him and that for less than a minute.

He said: "I covet no phraseology that lends respectability to sin. You can do a man so sorer injury than to lighten his conception of the awfulness of sin."

DR. R. A. TORREY

Dominantly earnest personality was his. Marvellous evangelist and prolific author.

He said: "Nothing lies beyond the reach of prayer except that which lies beyond the will of God. Prayer is the only omnipotence God grants a human being."

DR. LOUISE YIM

President, Central University, Seoul, Korea. A college with thousands of students. She headed the "under-ground movement" for Korea's independence, after Japan annexed Korea in 1910.

She spent eight years in a Japanese jail, living under threat of death each day and suffering unspeakable indignities at the hands of her captors.

She wrote a book, *My Forty Years' Fight for Korean Independence.* Great Christian woman of unusual intelligence and courage. The Japanese dragged her by the hair of her head down a street on one cruel occasion.

Sitting in the back pew of a church where she was all alone, her prayer was: "For my people. For my people. For peace."

SYNGMAN RHEE

President of South Korea. He was leader of the over-ground movement for the independence of Korea.

He spent eight years in a Japanese jail—suffering many tortures, wearing a thirty-pound yoke around his neck for twenty-two hours a day, having red hot needles thrust under his finger nails.

In the jail one day—in great physical torture and soul agony, he cried aloud: "O God, save my soul and my country!" God saved him then and there. Before his prison life ended, he had led forty-two guards and inmates of the jail to faith in Christ. He told me: "Tell your people back home to watch out for Communism in the schools— yes, and even in the churches. Communism and Christianity cannot co-exist. We do not try to co-exist with cholera."

DR. BYRON HOOVER DEMENT

First president of Baptist Bible Institute, New Orleans. A Sir Galahad of God he in church and educational areas and arenas. I had the joy and honor to be his pastor when I was pastor of the First Baptist Church, New Orleans.

Once he wrote me a letter, and, with wit and humor, signed it this way: "Byron (not Lord) Hoover (not president) Dement (not Ed)."

DR. JOHN ROACH STRATTON

A consecrated contender for the "faith once delivered" was he. A feared antagonist. Pastor of Calvary Baptist Church, New York City. He said: "Either God is weak, or a fool, or immoral if he does not have a hell for violators of his righteous laws."

GOVERNOR HUEY LONG OF LOUISIANA

Once I did the preaching in a revival meeting at First Baptist Church, Shreveport, Louisiana, Dr. M. E. Dodd, pastor. I visited Huey

Long in his office. I asked him: "Are you a Christian?" He answered: "Yes. But few people believe I am. But if believing that Jesus Christ is the Son of God, that he came and died on the cross of Calvary and was buried and rose again—and if trusting him to save my soul, makes me a Christian, then I am one, and I am a Baptist, as is my mother."

I said: "Well, then, if you are saved and are a Baptist, you ought to place your membership in the First Baptist Church." He stared at me, his eyes sparkling.

He said: "Join that hypocritical ice house? Why, old man Thomas is a member there, and he hates me. And he is insulting the intelligence of the citizens of Louisiana by running to be governor. Every time he makes a speech, he gets ten thousand votes away from the governor's chair."

After some other conversation, he promised me to come to place his membership in the First Baptist Church the following Sunday, saying, "Old Thomas will walk out when I join."

The following Sunday, when I gave the invitation, about forty people came to present themselves for membership, among them was Huey Long.

And when he was governor, impeachment proceedings were brought against him. The House of Representatives lodged nineteen charges against him. Huey Long needed fourteen senators to block conviction.

Fifteen senators signed a "round robin" return stating that as a result of legal irregularities, they would not vote to remove Governor Long no matter what the evidence might show. After the round robin the remaining twenty-four members of the Senate realized they had been defeated. Whereupon the Senate adjourned and the impeachment was dead.

SENATOR STROM THURMOND OF SOUTH CAROLINA

When I was pastor of the First Baptist Church, Edgefield, South Carolina, I was his pastor. I baptized his twin sisters—Martha and Mary.

Senator Strom Thurmond has been a farmer, lawyer, schoolteacher, athletic coach, school superintendent, state senator, judge, governor,

United States Senator and presidential candidate.

A veteran of World War II and a Major General in the U.S. Army Reserve, Senator Thurmond has been awarded eighteen decorations, medals, and awards, including the Legion of Merit, Bronze Star with "V," Purple Heart, Belgian Order of The Crown, and French *Croix de Guerre.*

He was elected to the United States Senate in 1954 in a write-in campaign—the first person ever elected to a major office in the United States by this method. He was reelected twice as a Democrat and once as a Republican.

The senator is noted for his history-making predictions and achievements, his independence, adherence to Constitutional principles, economy in government, and his strong support of military preparedness.

In 1957, he delivered the longest speech ever made in the United States Senate (24 hours, 18 minutes). It was in defense of jury trials.

In 1961, he coined the phrase "no-win" foreign policy and warned that such a policy is based on the fallacious notion that Communist leaders are softening.

In January, 1962, he warned that Soviet missiles were in Cuba nearly a year before the Administration took action. In 1968, he authored the federal anti-riot law.

TY COBB

Baseball notable, who had a batting average of .367 for twenty-four years.

This is what he did on one May day as playing-manager of the Detroit Tigers. I forget the year, but this is what a St. Louis newspaper published:

Cobb poled out three homers in today's game with the St. Louis Browns. They were off pitchers Bush, Vangilder, and Gaston. Cobb, in smashing out six hits, collected sixteen bases, a new world's record for modern major league baseball. His three homers tied the record for this specialty in modern major league baseball and he also collected a double and two singles.

In one of the few conversations I had with him, he said to me: "I am not as mean as some sports writers say I am. I sit on the edge of the dugout sometimes and sharpen my shoe spikes so that the fellows who play against me can see me. When I try to steal second, no second baseman ought to get in my way."

HONORABLE JAMES BYRNES

Secretary of State was he, the man Franklin D. Roosevelt called his "assistant president." Byrnes held posts in almost every field of government. He was an associate justice of the United States Supreme Court, Secretary of State, United States Representative, United States Senator, director of economic stabilization and war mobilization during World War II, a delegate to the United Nations General Assembly and governor of South Carolina.

In Key Biscayne, Florida, President Nixon ordered the flag over the White House flown at half-mast when Byrnes died. "He was a great man who always put his country ahead of his party," the President said.

Born in Charleston, South Carolina, Byrnes went to work at an early age to help his widowed mother. Byrnes' political career began in 1910 when he scored a 57-vote upset victory over a veteran representative. He later said he ran "on nerve and nerve alone." Looking back over his public service career he said in later years, "There are two happy days in the life of a man in public office—the day he is elected and the day he steps out."

President Roosevelt appointed Byrnes to the United States Supreme Court in 1941, but Byrnes held the post for only one year.

Byrnes went to the Democratic National Convention in 1944 as a candidate for the vice-presidential nomination. But Roosevelt advised that a Southern running mate would hurt his chances for reelection, asked him to step aside. Byrnes did and Harry S. Truman was nominated. Byrnes remained in public service almost continuously, however. He was with Roosevelt at Yalta and Truman at Potsdam.

MAX PALMER

I met and ate lunch with him in a Bible conference in Bowling Green, Kentucky, where and when he and I were speakers.

Max was a giant—eight feet tall. He weighed 425 pounds. He was a great athlete. Playing basketball, he averaged seventy-eight points per game, for many games. He was offered four million dollars for a ten-year contract, but a physical injury incapacitated him. He made millions of dollars as a wrestler and a movie star.

Then liquor got the best of the giant. After some years of dissipated living, he became a Christian and has spoken on Christian subjects all over our land. A miracle of God's regenerative grace.

SERGEANT ALVIN YORK

He spent some hours in my office. He expressed appreciation of a sermon he heard me preach. He spoke to me of war as a "wanton horror." He won the Medal of Honor—the nation's highest military decoration—in the waning days of World War I. He died in 1964.

GEORGE WASHINGTON CARVER

A black scientist he. He made many important contributions to mankind that will long be remembered. He was born in slavery in Diamond, Missouri, in 1864. He died in 1943. He overcame many obstacles to get an education. Often he was called "The Negro Pasteur" and sometimes "The Peanut Man" because of his genius in extracting three hundred products from the common peanut. During his lifetime, he was the recipient of many awards.

In 1947, a few years after his death, the United States Post Office printed a three-cent postage stamp in honor of him, and his birthplace was declared a national monument.

He was not spoiled as a result of fame nor was he tempted to leave Tuskegee Institute because of the opportunity to earn more money.

GOVERNOR PAT NEFF

Governor of Texas. He was sometimes called "the handsomest man in all of Texas." His appeal to all classes was most effectively extraordinary.

When he was president of Baylor University, he invited me to come and "preach a week." He said he did not want a "religious emphasis week" but "a week of "sho-nuff" gospel preaching." I asked him to tell me about the greatest day of his life. He said, "Aside from the day I was saved, it was the day when I brought my mother from a humble house on the plains to the governor's mansion."

JOE JACKSON

He was a baseball player with the Chicago White Sox. When he was involved in the scandal of throwing a game in the World Series, a little boy to whom Joe was a hero high among heroes, said, with a broken heart and a sobbing voice: "Say it ain't so, Joe! Say it ain't so."

Once I ate "set-up" breakfast with the man whom Ty Cobb described as "the greatest natural hitter of any man who ever used a baseball bat."

Joe played in his sock feet or barefooted. That is why he was called "Shoeless Joe." One day he came in from the outfield fussing furiously. He said: "Glass in that outfield. Glass out there." "Cutting your feet, Joe?" asked his manager.

"No," he said, "but that glass is roughing up that ball, something terrible."

DR. LEN G. BROUGHTON

Born in a log cabin in North Carolina. It is no disparagement of any other preacher I have heard to say that to me he was the greatest preacher I ever heard. He was a strong premillennial preacher. People listened to him like children frightened at a storm or like slaves to an emancipation proclamation.

Congregations, listening to him, became a human pendulum between smiles and tears.

Every drop of his blood was courageous blood. Small of stature was he. Sam Jones, the nationally famous evangelist, once presented him to a large audience, saying: "I present to you Len Broughton. He weighs a hundred and four pounds—four pounds of hair and one hundred pounds of backbone."

When he died, it was as if a giant tree had fallen in the forest and left a great vacancy against the sky. Wonderful educationally and spiritually the ten days I roomed with him when we spoke at a Baptist Assembly in DeLand, Florida—"away back yonder."

GOVERNOR JIMMY DAVIS

In his youth a country boy. I first met him on the campus at

Louisiana State University. I was preaching in a revival meeting in Baton Rouge. After we had talked and made remarks about the weather, I asked: "Jimmie, if God called you today would you be ready?"

He said: "I hope God doesn't call me."

"But if he did, would you be ready?" I asked again.

He answered not a word. But that night Jimmie came to hear me preach—his greatest interest being to see what sort of vocabulary was mine in using the English language.

That night, the Holy Spirit worked. Jimmie came forward eagerly, accepting Jesus as his Savior.

Twice he made me colonel on his staff: once in his first term as governor of Louisiana, the next in his second term. A great statesman and Christian is he, singing his way with gospel hymns into the hearts of millions. Great and grateful are the memories I have of the two days and nights Mrs. Lee and I spent in the governor's mansion.

Jimmy, though still living, is enshrined in the Country Music Hall of Fame at Nashville.

Jimmy is best known for the country classic, "You Are My Sunshine," which he composed.

PETE GRAY

Once he attended the Business Men's Bible Class at Bellevue Baptist Church—the only time I ever spoke to him. Born in Nanticoke, Pennsylvania. Pete was *a one-armed outfielder* who played with the Memphis Chicks and went from there to the Major Leagues, playing with the St. Louis Browns in 1945.

Twenty-eight years old, he batted left, threw left, caught left. He appeared in seventy-seven games, batting .218. In 51 games he batted .234.

Pete Gray asked no favors and resented any special treatment. In a sandlot game, he once slid so hard into home plate that he knocked the ball out of the catcher's grasp. "If it wasn't for your handicap, I'd bust your face in," the catcher said to Gray. Pete didn't wait. He took one swing at the catcher and knocked him down. "What handicap?" he said.

In 1944, Pete Gray did it all in the Southern League. He batted .333. He collected 119 hits for 221 total bases and drove in 60 runs—not bad for batting second most of the season. He hit five home runs—two of them out of the ballpark, the other three inside the park. He stole 68 bases, tying the record set fifteen years earlier by KiKi Cuyler.

DR. A. J. BARTON

He has been dead for years. But he still lives, because of the influence he had on my life.

Head of the Social Service Commission of the Southern Baptist Convention, he was a man of stature and influence among Southern Baptists and with presidents of the United States. Mighty in intellect, he was sweet-spirited and humble.

Our little eight-year-old daughter had often said to my wife and me: "I am never going to marry and leave you."

After Dr. Barton spent some hours in our home in New Orleans and after he had eaten at our table, she said: "Daddy, I have changed my mind about this thing of getting married. I am going to marry Dr. Barton."

GYPSY SMITH

Born in a gypsy tent, reared as a gypsy boy, unable to read at fourteen, this man became world-renowned as an evangelist. Kings and queens invited him to their palaces and tables.

I first met him in Allentown, Pennsylvania, where he visited his friend Oliver Kufer who was my sweetly great and greatly sweet friend. It was by chance I ran upon him and his young bride in the lobby of a hotel, where they were spending some days on their honeymoon. He asked me to eat breakfast with him and his bride. I did so. In one conversation I spoke of his influence and renown in the world. He said: "If I have any influence and renown, it is because of Jesus who made himself of no reputation and took upon himself the form of a servant." He told me that before Jesus came or before death came, he wanted to preach a week in the Bellevue Baptist Church. We made the engagement. But on his voyage back from Liverpool to America, he died at sea. And thus my pastorate was robbed of great joy and blessing.

BILLY SUNDAY

One man like Billy Sunday is about all God makes in a hundred years. I preached on the same platform with him on occasions—at Winona Lake Bible Conference. Billy knew Jesus with reverent familiarity and was deeply devoted. He was kind and gracious to me.

One Sunday afternoon in his home at Winona Lake, I found him restlessly pacing the floor, asking, "Are the folks coming?" He was to preach that afternoon. I said: "Yes, Billy, you are going to have a big crowd." He said: "Lord Jesus, help me so that the folks won't find an empty trough." I said: "Billy, I heard you say once that it would be as impossible for liquor to come back legally under the Stars and Stripes as it would be for a tom cat to run through a stove pipe with a sack of cement tied to its tail."

"Yes," he said, "I said it, and I never expected the American people to be such fools as to legalize the hellish traffic."

Then he began to speak as though he were addressing ten thousand people, when I was his only audience. I interrupted his fiery message by saying: "Billy, I don't drink booze."

"Oh, yes," he said, and he quieted down and asked me to pray for him since within an hour he would be preaching to a vast throng— and preaching, as always he did, for verdicts.

MAHALIA JACKSON

I first saw and met her at a black Baptist Church in New Orleans one Sunday afternoon. I had preached to an enthusiastic congregation who gave many amens to many of my assertions.

I was ready to go. The pastor: "Wait a few minutes, Doctor. I want you to hear a little black angel sing." I sat in a pew and listened to the little, plump, round-faced girl sing. Her voice and the hymn she sang blessed me.

Years later—in a Paris opera house—I heard her sing to an audience of three thousand. Just old gospel hymns she sang. When she finished an hour of singing, the applause she received was amazing. She had exalted Jesus in all she sang and in the way she sang.

When she died—in 1972, I believe—she was buried in New Orleans where she was born physically and born again spiritually.

Once she was offered $25,000 a week to sing in a night club in Las Vegas. Quickly she refused, saying, "I never sing where they serve liquor." There have been many banquets in many cities where she could not have sung because of liquor.

BABE RUTH

Once in St. Louis, my wife and I and our little seven-year-old daughter attended a baseball game. We were close to the gate where the players came in. When the great home-run hitter came in, our little daughter ran to him, took him by the hand, and asked for his autograph.

The strong athlete was as gentle with her as a mother. He sat down on a nearby bench, picked her up and put her on his knee, talked a bit with her, and gave his autograph. She has that autograph in a scrapbook today under plastic protection. Gentleness and strength were manifested by the great "Bambino." Gentleness made him great that day.

WILLIS HOTCHKISS

I was in my office one day years ago. I heard a light knock on the door between my office and the hall. Opening the door, I saw a sunburned, white-haired man, with eagle-like eyes, holding his hat in his left hand. He said softly, "Good day." I said, "Good day." Then he said, "I am Willis Hotchkiss." I said: "Oh! Dr. Hotchkiss, come in! Come in! I have wanted to see you since I was a boy. Sit down."

After a few minutes of conversation, he asked, "Why did you want to see me since you were a boy?"

I said: "I wanted to see the man who worked nearly three years to find one word in the language of an African tribe—the word that meant Savior."

"Yes," gently he said, "I worked three years to get that word—sometimes sleeping on dirt floors or vermin-infested straw, and eating rotten rhinoceros meat in my hunger. And I suffered several attacks of African fever. But after I found the word, I led many to trust in Christ."

I sat with greatness in my office that day.

PRIME MINISTER NEHRU

On my preaching mission to India, I prayed God to let me have an interview with the notable man of India. God graciously granted my prayerful request.

I went to my room one night at the New Delhi Hotel. I found an envelope with a sort of royal insigna. The card inside the envelope stated that the Prime Minister would see me at eight A.M. the next day. With Dr. Rao, the great Baptist preacher of India, appointed in 1973 by the lady Prime Minister of India, to a place of high authority, I took a cab for Nehru's mansion, evaluating greatly the permit in my hand.

The guards at the gate to the Prime Minister's estate demanded of me to tell why I was there. I showed them my permit. Like demand the guards at the door of the palace made of me. I showed them my permit. The door was opened, and I went in.

The Prime Minister came out into the living room. I had ten minutes with him. I told him I knew about his distress because the Chinese army had come over the mountains and was sitting on the top of his nation. But I said: "Sir, I pray for you. I know many Christians who pray for you. But we always pray in the name of Jesus—Son of man without sin, Son of God with power—the only hope for the welfare of your nation and of all nations—the only hope for the welfare of all people in Time and Eternity."

I told him other things about Jesus. He said: "Thank you, sir. That sounds good. Thank you, Sir!"

I talked with the lady who is now Prime Minister of India—for at least fifteen minutes. She mentioned how hunger was the haunting horror of India—and it still is.

RALPH CONNER

That is the nom de plume of a great author and preacher—a Reverend Gordon. He wrote many books. One book which he wrote—*The Sky Pilot*—has influenced my life more than any book I ever read except the Bible, the book divinely-inspired in totality, the miracle book of diversity in unity, of harmony in infinite complexity. I have read *The Sky Pilot* twice a year since, when I was sixteen, the book was given to me by a young woman of most excellent intelligence and Christian character.

I made a journey of one hundred and fifty miles to see and shake hands with Ralph Conner. An indescribable thrill went through my body when I held the hand that held the pen that wrote *The Sky Pilot*. What power has the printed page!

10.
Evolution

This is a copy of a letter I sent to a college student who told me that "a certain professor held up to scorn all who do not believe in evolution."

Dear Friend: I have your letter of recent date asking me concerning your acceptance or refusal of Charles Darwin's "Theory of Organic Evolution." If you want to be wise and sensible and scholarly, don't drink one drop from this polluted reservoir of such nonsense as Darwin put forth in his theory of evolution. It is 100% theory—and never any fact about it. You can no more believe the Bible and Darwin's theory of evolution than you can be a man and a woman at the same time. Young people have asked me if anybody could be a Christian and be an evolutionist. To this, I want to tell you what Dr. E. Schuyler English said:

"You can not be an *informed* Christian and a *logical* evolutionist. We need to awake to the horrible implications of evolution and its denial of the truth of God. The cardinal truth for the Christian is that man was created in the image of God; man fell from his state of innocency and sinlessness; and man, apart from God's provision in His Son, is lost. The Atonement was necessary for man's salvation.

"The essence of Evolution is that man developed slowly from a speck of protoplasm in the sea; man has not fallen; man has followed an upward course from protoplasm to monkey, from monkey to the man, from tree-man to the creature of the Stone Age and Bronze Age, etc.; there was no fall; there was rise; there was no need for atonement, for man has not sinned against God; man is still an *unfinished* creature, still evolving.

"How can a person logically believe at the same time that man was created in the image of God and that he came into being out of a bit of protoplasm in the ocean? How can a person possibly hold *concurrently* that man was created perfect and fell—and that man never fell, is still imperfect, still rising?

"How can a person possibly believe *coincidentally that* man, being a sinner, needed that atonement be made for his sins—and that man has never sinned against God and therefore needs no atoning sacrifice? To say that evolution is embraced in the doctrines of Christianity is to say that black is white, untruth is truth, solid is liquid, a bird is a fish.

"No logical evolutionist can be a Christian. No true, informed Christian will remain long in evolution."

An abiding conviction of my soul is that back of much of the moral looseness that has manifested itself in criminality in our nation and in our community is the infernal, ignorant, abominable, blasphemous, blatant, devilish, erroneous, foolish, hellish, iniquitous, supercilious, subtle theory of Evolution that has gotten abroad in the school and college life in vast areas.

To whom can the evolutionist pray? Since in him resides all the power there can be for progress and since by inherent forces he has fought his way through all the lower forms of life, what efficacy can there be in praying to God, if there is one, who has either been helpless in or indifferent to his struggles thus far? If God could not or would not help me to become man, then I have no use for Him now that I am man. If I, through countless ages, could lift myself from the amoeba to my present complex physical organization and form and my multiform mental and moral powers, then I can dispense with God altogether and can continue without His help or interference to lift myself by myself from human to superhuman; from superhuman to God; from God to super-God. There is no place in the evolutionist's scheme of things for and no need of an omnipotent God.

"In the beginning God created." The spiritual blindness of first century heathenism is equalled, if not surpassed, by the blindness of modern heathenism. There is no contest between genuine science and revelation. But science is the study of facts. Evolution is a juggling with guesses.

The Bible and evolution, the Bible revelation and evolution, are utterly and irreconcilably opposed to one another. They are two express trains, dashing 70 miles an hour in opposite directions. Between revelation and evolution, the Bible and evolution, there is a great gulf fixed, wider than the ablest apologist can hope to bridge.

Man can't believe in both any more than he can carry water and fire in the same bucket—any more than he can be dead and alive, awake and asleep, at the same time. Evolution is the antithesis of Christianity! If the Bible is true, Evolution cannot be true.

Evolution is the theory that from a nebulous mass of primeval substance, whose origin we cannot account for, there came by natural processes all we see and know in the heavens above and the earth beneath—the ignoble forms of life, the animalcular and animal life, not only the exquisite mechanisms of the human body, but the human mind, with its emotions and intellect, will, and all their phenomena, were latent in the fiery cloud! In other words, evolution is the doctrine that this life of man, this moral, this ethical, spiritual nature, has been developed by natural processes—that man has come, not complete from the hand of God—that all things came by continuous progressive changes, according to certain laws, by means of resident forces—that everything—all things—started from a single cell, which came from no one knows where, all that exists evolved—trees, plants, insects, birds, beasts, and man—and this first cell has no external aid from any source whatever.

But I am here to say, on the authority of the Bible, that the beginning of all things, the differentiations of all forms of life, and the orderly changes of nature, all are defined by the one word CREATION and none of them are rightly defined by the word evolution!

Never until scientists dismiss the false theory of all things evolving by natural causes and processes and grasp the truth "in the beginning God," and of God's creative program with continuous orderly change, will they rightly interpret the facts of nature, or have a sound basis for scientific research and development. As man's involuntary functional acts, so God's persistent cosmical activities, by which nature is produced and sustained, are as much a part of his manifestation as are his purposeful expressions of love, justice, and wisdom!

Man's physical nature did not evolve from brute ancestors. It was a distinct creation capable of expressing spiritual qualities not found in any animal.

Man's spiritual nature did not evolve. God breathed into him, and he became a living soul. Man's idea of God, divine law, and religious aspirations did not evolve. They were created by divine revelation and inspiration. Christianity did not evolve. It is a creation by the manifestation of the incarnate Son of God redeeming, regenerating, and indwelling man by man's faith, and expressing himself in and through man. Theory of organic evolution did not evolve. It was created in the darkened minds of unspiritual men to account for nature without God. Theistic theory of evolution did not evolve. Created by theologians to harmonize with the theory of organic evolution.

Evolution versus Bible account of man.—Did man descend from the brute or was he divinely created? Specially created! This is the question in a nutshell!

Evolution's account accepted substantially by all evolutionists: "Man descended from a hairy quadruped, furnished with a tail and pointed ears, probably arborial in its habits and an inhabitant of the Old World. This creature, if its whole structure had been examined by a naturalist, would have been classed among the Quadrumana, as surely as would the common and still more ancient progenitor of the Old and New World monkeys. The Quadrumana and all the higher mammals are probably derived from an ancient marsupial animal, and this through a long line of diversified forms either from some reptile-like, or some amphibian-like creature, and this again from some fish-like animal. In the dim obscurity of the past, we can see that the early progenitor of the Vertebrate must have been an aquatic animal, provided with branchia, with the two sexes united in the same individual!"

Bible account: "And God said, Let us make man in our image, after our likeness: and let them have dominion over the fish of the sea, and over the fowl of the air, and over all the earth. So God created man in his own image, in the image of God created he him;

male and female created he them." "And the Lord formed man of
the dust of the ground and breathed into his nostrils the breath of
life; and man became a living soul."

Yet this is called science, scholarship, wisdom, and those who do
not prefer this to Genesis' account are called "old fogey" and "ignorant."

Evolution versus Bible account of the universe.—Evolution originated
in heathenism and ends in atheism. It is violently opposed to the
narrative and doctrines of the Bible and destructive of all Christian
faith. In nothing is this more evidently seen than in its account of
the creation of the universe. It is simply a revamping of the old doctrine
of chance clothed in scientific terms.

Evolution leaves no room for a Creator. It excludes entirely supernatural process, every prearranged and conscious acts of a personal
character. It is the nonmiraculous theory of creation. Evolution turns
the Creator out of doors. Infidels all accept it gladly. Every atheist
is an evolutionist.

Evolution fails to account for the origin of matter. Everything came
from a cell. "A single cell in the midst of chaos accounts for all."
But who put the cell there? "The ultimate atom!" But who is the
father of that ultimate atom? The origin of matter, the first and
fundamental fact of creation, is not solved by evolution! There is
no other account conceivable than that the Bible gives "In the beginning, God created."

There is not the slightest evidence that living matter could arise
from non-living matter. Living matter cannot come from dead matter
by any process—only a "scientific desperado" dares assert that life
came from dead matter, or that all scholars accept evolution. So
evolution fails at the start in the story of life. Yet this is its chosen
field. On this depends the whole theory. If there was a cause at the
origin of life, why not at the origin of all living things? It is simply
a question of degree. The making of a single cell, the simplest creature that lives, is as great a mystery as that of man. Conceptually
the one is as possible as the other!

Evolution does not account for the orderly movements of the heavenly bodies which have the accuracy of a chronomete.—which are the standards by which all chronometers are regulated, so that the astronomers can calculate to a second when the heavenly bodies shall pass any particular point or form their many conjuctions. There is no collision. There is no noise.

Our solar system is unique in the heavens. The earth's situation is far enough from the sun to be beyond its powerful heat and electric energy and yet near enough to preserve and continue all life. The arrangement of its surface into land and water proportions gives the requisite amount of moisture over the land areas. The atmosphere is mixed gases in just the right proportion for life. Watch our solar system at work. It is unthinkable that planets could get together and decide on their own laws. All this speaks as loudly as any mechanism can speak, of intention and benevolence and control and careful adjustment—far from that haphazard effect which comes from the undirected working of "resident forces"!

"Matter and force achieve all things!" Wow! Blind force and the milling of atoms had combined all the happy adjustments of the universe. What a miracle! Throw newspaper type against the wall and get newspapers printed and folded. Blind force brought to pass the countless millions of far more wonderful arrangements, such as the eye, the hand, the humming bird's wing, the bull-bat's mouth? Who could believe the unsmeltered ore in the mountains could, by blind force, bring forth an Elgin watch? How much less then can we conceive of blind force and feelingless matter bringing forth such marvels as the eye, the brain, reason, love, memory? These things are not in matter. How then can they come from matter? Is there thought in a brick? Love in a rock? Love in a thorn tree?

The evolutionist's task is to find in the less than 100 material elements of life, reason, love, imagination, will, thought, genius, law, design, beauty, music, color, laughter, logic, instinct, and the soul, not one of which is in matter. The greater cannot come from the lesser. The universe is either the work of Infinite power and Intelligence, or it is the result of blind, unaided force—chance! "Order and not chaos is the law of the universe." "In the world of law there is no place for caprice." A spiritual creator and not chanced evolution is the cause of the universe.

Evolution is not scientific. It has not been proven to be true. Is that Science which makes an unproven theory the basis of all modern thinking, the foundation of a universal philosophy, the cause of a revolution in theology, the reason for the rejecting the narratives of the Bible, and, on the part of some, of abandoning Christianity and launching into atheism? Is it scientific to accept as true an unproven theory and make it the basis of all belief? Not at all. Is that scientific which rests upon circumstantial evidence which in law is least relied upon and on which evidence innocent men have been hung? Shall we condemn the whole race to bestial origin in the same evidence? Shall we suspend the philosophy of the universe upon a few hairs? Shall we allow the guess as to the tip of the outer ear to revolutionize theology? Shall we risk our eternal destiny on the supposed uselessness of the so-called gill slits in premature puppies?

Yet this is the demand of evolution reduced to plain English. And that is called Science, scholarship! If evolution is Science, why did Darwin use the words "we may well suppose" more than 800 times in his printed works? How would it sound to say "we may well suppose the sun is shining, we may well suppose that snow falls in winter, we may well suppose the sea exists"?

Every real scientist knows that science begins with observed facts, and works from the known to discover the unknown. Science is still experimenting in the realm of secondary causes and effects. It reveals nothing primal or ultimate.

Is that a Science against which the highest scholarship of the world is arrayed? Is that Science which has not a single demonstrated fact to support it? It that a Science worthy one minute's consideration which says that a female ape became a woman? Contrast the hairy, brutish beast, soul-less, senseless, with the glory and perfection of woman's form and face, to say nothing of her soul, nature, and mind. I could believe that a rock, or a turtle could sing the national anthem sooner than I could accept such a theory.

Can Evolution account for Christ? Evolution cannot account for

Christ. Without entering on an argument for his divinity, we simply present him and ask the evolutionist to account for such a character and life. To say that Jesus was an evolution of the age in which he lived, as some evolutionists do say, and that we may look for even a greater in the future, is to be guilty, not only of blasphemy but of gross ignorance as to the age in which Jesus came. There was nothing in that age to give rise to such a character. He came as a flash of lightning in a dark sky, or, according to the Bible figure, as the rising of the sun in the world's night. Neither science nor religion can support a lie without giving it power to do evil!

It would require a large volume to reveal the evil effects of the evolutionary theory to date. It is credited with having been highly influential in producing the psychological conditions that brought on the World War. Carried to its logical conclusion, the doctrine of the survival of the fittest makes war the inevitable means of deciding what nations and peoples shall dominate. Its philosophy is the opposite of Christ's program of love, sacrifice, and service, as the means of highest attainment, for men and nations.

The progressive acceptance of the theory of organic evolution has resulted in a corresponding decline of faith in the supernatural origin and character of Christianity—also in the substitution of a purely cultural, natural, humanitarianism social service system of ethics, lacking all that is distinctly Christian, and incapable of accomplishing the purposes of Christianity. The whole anti-Christ movement within the world is the outgrowth of applying the Evolutionary theory and philosophy to divine revelation and Christian experience. It denies revealed truth in the name of Science and scholarship. It substitutes a theory that is neither scientific nor scholarly. Search America from ocean to ocean and you will not find one scientist, teacher, or preacher, engaged in disseminating this false knowledge, who knows God experientially, or is scientific in his attitude toward Jesus Christ.

Evolution professing great wisdom is propagating a naturalism that does not explain nature; propagating a rationalism that is irrational, a theory of science that is unscientific, a philosophy that is without a proven premise or an ultimate conclusion, a theology that dishonors

God, a theology that belittles Jesus Christ, a theory that exalts the human ego, a false knowledge that is utterly ineffective as a means to spiritual progress.

This anti-Christ theory has made puppets of near-scientists and used them to disseminate materialism. It has made monkeys of agnostic teachers, and induced them to chatter to youth about their simian ancestors. It has made owls of materialistic journalists, and keeps them hooting about natural laws, and evolution explaining everything. It has made donkeys of schoolmade preachers and set them to braying about "higher values," "ethical culture," "human service," and "the ideals of Jesus," while denying his divine origin and nature, the validity of his miracles, and the efficacy of his atonement; the fact of his resurrection, and his gift of life eternal through blood sacrifice. I can't help but believe when these who so do really know Christ, they will turn from this unproven theory as from a venomous serpent.

This anti-Christ theory and theology appeals to the human ego, with: "Come on, fellows, let's destroy the Old Book, and build us a modern church founded on the ideals of Jesus and the new knowledge of science. We will accept the sayings of Jesus insofar as they agree with our thinking but reject his Deity, vicarious atonement, resurrection, and all else that is supernatural."

No God-taught soul can be an evolutionist. Whoever knows the Creator believes in creation and in Divine revelation. Scholarly agnosticism and intellectural egotism are not signs of advanced, scientific knowledge, but proof of ignorance of spiritual realities.

The betrayed dupes of anti-Christ that substitute ethical culture and humanitarianism for regeneration and Christian service, are under the illusion that they constitute the advance guard of a new-age religion. Whereas the truth is, they have lost the way. They are in a mental fog that hinders and prevents spiritual perception. They have unwittingly become false prophets, betraying those who receive their teaching! Whatever good may be claimed for the theory, evolution is both unscientific and unchristian. It is incapable of producing a high degree of morals, or of sustaining a righteous civilization.

Imagine what would become of American institutions and ideals if all citizens accepted what thousands of college-trained men and women are accepting; ie., that man is a super-brutal creature, that religion is superstitution; that there is no God and no life after death, no authority but custom, and no rule of conduct but expediency. Let the advocates of this false philosophy ponder this question, then answer their conscience and to the rising generation.

The statesmen who laid the foundation of the American government made Christianity the chief cornerstone. Today this cornerstone is being undermined by educational institutions that they made possible. The Word of God, in which they put their trust, is now ridiculed by the beneficiaries of their sacrifices. The faith in God that gave them victory is fast being supplanted by faith in a godless theory that threatens to defeat national righteousness.

When men, betrayed by false thinking, no longer believe in Divine authority; when they no longer respect the sacredness of virtue, marriage and parentage; when cold, calculating intelligence, unrestrained by religious conviction, controls conduct; then national honor is doomed.

Christian principles are fundamental to righteous citizenship and government. Materialism and infidelity, clothed with the responsibility of science and rationalism, have combined to destroy faith in the supernatural, in the reality of things spiritual, and in the verities of vital Christianity.

Evolution stands at the bar—the bar of true science, the bar of true philosophy, the bar of human history, the bar of geological facts, the bar of God's revelation, the bar of mercy. Truth is at once the accuser and the judge. The judge says to the accused, You have been tried and found guilty. You are a criminal, an outlaw. I am the court of final appeal. In the presence of all mankind and the Maker of heaven and earth, I condemn you.

In the name of science—the facts are against you. In the name of philosophy—reason is against you. In the name of history—you have wrought much evil. In the name of the Bible—you are at war with it. In the name of the church—you are weakening and hindering it. In the name of a great army of students—you are destroying their faith in a living, personal God and standing them in the sea at the very beginning of their voyage. In the name of thousands of parents whose hearts you have broken, and whose fondest hopes for their sons and daughters you have blasted forever. In the name of the brave boys who fell in the great war, whose blood you spilled without mercy and whose lives you took without pay. In the name of homes which you have broken, of orphans you have made destitute, of fathers whom you have cast into early graves, of mothers whose bitter tears you have caused to flow. In the name of the coming generation, whose godly faith, highest hopes and most noble aspirations, you stand ready to destroy.

I condemn it and hate it because it hides the presence of God—it calls for no repentance or consecration, it boasts of human progress and claims merit therefor. It is the worship of man rather than the worship of God. It deifies man and ignores Christ. It has no explanation for Christian experience. Because once committed to this theory there is no extreme the person may not reach. Some have abandoned Christ and Christianity because of it. It is in fact, in doctrine, in experience, the opposite of Christianity. It dissipates any looking for supernatural changes such as the last Day, the coming of Christ, and the resurrection. It removes that wholesome fear of God so operative in deterring evil and stimulating good. The most absurd of all absurdities parading under the guise of "scholarship" and "science"—using the livery of heaven to serve the devil in.

So, with all these words before you, I beg you, dear fellow, to refuse to believe the theory of evolution as firmly as you would refuse to let a rattlesnake into a kindergarten, as you would refuse to put sewerage water into your coffee, as you would refuse to make a tour through a powder factory with a flaming acetylene torch.

11.
"Tackhole" Lee

NOTE: I offer this as a vignette concerning my brother, Thomas Kirk-patrick Lee.

By Walton Lowry
Outdoor Editor, *The Birmingham News*

There's no doubt about it. Tackhole Lee shot his way into Alabama's Sports Hall of Fame.

Tom Jones, Irvine Porter, Clyde Sellers, and Dan Glenn, Jr., all standout Alabama gunners, firmly believe Tackhole was the greatest all-round shot that ever lived.

And Jimmy Robinson, *Sports Afield*, trap and skeet editor, tags Tackhole as one of, if not the best, in the business.

Thomas Kirkpatrick Lee, who got the nickname Tackhole, by tack right rifle groups at 100 yards, was born June 18, 1889, at Fort Mill, South Carolina.

While he hunted little, Lee made the South Carolina papers in 1907, by killing 49 birds with 51 shots.

In 1917, as commanding captain at Camp Perry, he was already a rifle, pistol, and shotgun phenom, having set a world rifle record in 1913 with 1999 x 2000 and later bettering that with a perfect score.

A few old timers can remember, way back forty odd years ago, when the old Birmingham Athletic Club used to stage "Society Circuses."

While Lee's sensational shooting acts, with the aid of his wife, always brought oohs and aahs, his most daring feat often brought little applause.

Why? Because the crowd didn't think it was possible. His wife would hold four buffalo nickel-size targets between her fingers.

Lee would place a shoe box on the barrel of his rifle so he couldn't see the sights. then he'd proceed to shoot them from between her fingers. The applause was often light because the crowd thought it was faked.

Lee designed and perfected the Lee Dot. This black dot on the crosshairs of a powerful scope shows up on a crow, or black animal, like a sooty spot on a lady's nose.

Immediately after World War I, Lee came to Birmingham and made his home until his death, August 9, 1957.

The Lee Dot is still super secret. Fact is, only Birmingham's Dan Glenn, Jr., who used to work with Lee, knows how to put such a dot on black widow spider "thread" so fine, it can't be seen with the naked eye.

Jones, skeet All-America, says Lee was so deadly with a trap gun when he first knew him, he'd have been afraid to let Lee shoot at him around a corner.

Sellers, state Smallbore Champ in 1941, and big bore champ in 1942, said: "Tackhole was great. Fact is, he was the hardest man to beat I ever shot against, and he would not have a gun unless it was in perfect condition. He was a legend when I was just a kid boy."

In addition to the famous "dot" for scopes, Lee was always experimenting with wildcat loads.

The Lee-Tomic load was one of these. It was a 25 calibre case, rolled down to take a .22 bullet, and travelled at 4500 feet per second. It was so "souped up" that it would explode when it hit the target.

As Porter points out, a number of great shooters could equal or top Lee in their specialty. But Lee was a whiz with shotgun, rifle, and pistol. Slow fire, rapid fire, skeet, trap, live pigeons or what have you.

Take a look at Lee's records and you'll see why he carted home more than 700 trophies.

And you'll see also why his standing offer of $15,000 side purse to meet any man in the world in a three-gun match was never challenged.

12.
"Leaving on a Smoke Train"

Those who suffer the torments of hay fever know how cigarette smoke is amazingly irritating. This happened before the days of special sections for smokers and nonsmokers.

For sixty years, hay fever has been a bunch of thorns in my body, especially in the regions of my nasal passage.

Things that cause me to sneeze—sometimes mildly, sometimes violently—are newsprint, shaving cream, feather pillows, fuzzy blankets, perfume, cat fur, dog hair, goldenrod pollen, dandruff, horse sweat, smoke from log-burnings. All of these are as tormenting to a hay fever victim as smoke in the eyes, as salt in a fresh cut or some member of the body.

On this "parlor" car were eighteen folks—all adults—five men and thirteen women. Two of the men were smoking and, to my amazement, all of the women! The car was cloudy with smoke. My hay fever nose began to sneeze. If all the sneezes I sneezed had been put in one big sneeze, it would have cracked my head.

A courteous and efficient black man wearing a white coat that somewhat increased the black gentleman look, came in. I, tormented, called to him and asked: "Look here, porter! Isn't there somewhere on this train a gentleman can get and not have to smell cigarette smoke?"

The porter scratched his head and thoughtfully answered: "Boss, the engineer, he ain't got no woman with him."

I think I have done little good in criticizing and rebuking women privately and publicly. I have said that a woman who smokes reminds me of a California bungalow—shingled all around, painted in front, and a small attic. God did not make people's noses to be smokestacks. If he had he would have made them out of brick and mortar and put them upon the top of their heads.

Turning from smoking women to smoking men, I say that a big man who is slave to a cigarette makes me think of a farmer who takes his hogs to market in a $15,000 limousine.

Sometimes I get tired of talking to people and of having them talk to me. The three hardest things I have to do is nothing, preach twenty minutes, and be a good conversationalist. I have sometimes been bored to the border of irritation by the talk I have to listen to. Sometimes I like to be silent and say nothing and listen to no voice.

Accordingly, once when I was on the train going to Allentown, Pennsylvania, where I went for a preaching mission at Waldheim Park, I told my Lady Lee that I was going to try to go to Allentown and have no conversation with anybody.

At the railroad station, the little lady ticket seller, who knew me, asked if I was well. I bobbed my head, but said nothing. At the St. Louis station, I pointed the red cap to my luggage and put some money in his outstretched hand without speaking a word.

In the diner, as I ate breakfast between St. Louis and Indianapolis, I pointed to the foods listed on the menu card, but not a word did I say.

After breakfast, I went to my seat in the Pullman car. Just out of St. Louis a man came in and sat down beside me. He wore a clergyman's collar. That did not bother me. If he wanted to go forward into his collar while I backed into mine, did not disturb me.

After some minutes, the stranger said to me: "Howdy do."

I said, "Howdy."

Then he, with a sort of hesitant boldness, asked: "What are you?"

"A priest" I answered.

"You are not dressed like a priest," he said.

"No," said I, "clothes do not make a preacher. Benedict Arnold had on his country's uniform when he betrayed his country."

There was a long pause.

"And I am a king, too." I said. "I don't wear a crown and I don't sit on a throne and live in a mansion, but I am a king."

"Where do you get all that stuff," he asked with some discourtesy.

I had my New Testament in my hand. I turned to Revelation, the first chapter, verses five and six: "Unto him who loved us, and washed us from our sins . . . and hath made us kings and priests unto God and his Father; to him be glory and dominion for ever and ever. Amen!"

He said: "Oh, I see. You are a Baptist preacher!"

"Yes," said I, intending to break off the conversation.

"Well, I guess you are one of those 'kiver to kiver' preachers," he said, a sort of scorn in his words.

"If you mean by those words that I believe the Bible to be the inspired, infallible, inerrant word of God, you have it right," I said.

"Which means you believe that legend about Adam and Eve?" he asked.

"Yes, I believe what the Bible says about the first man and the first woman, but it is not a legend or a myth." Then he declared, with an air of superiority, that he was an evolutionist and that Adam came to be by a process of evolution and not by a direct creative act of God.

Then I forgot my intention when I left home not to talk. This stranger said strongly, almost vehemently, that man was in "the family line of the monkey, and had strong resemblance to such an animal." He laughed to scorn this account in Genesis:

And the Lord God caused a deep sleep to fall upon Adam, and he slept: and he took one of his ribs, and closed up the flesh instead thereof; and the rib, which the Lord God had taken from man, made he a woman, and brought her unto the man" (Gen. 2:21-22).

At this time, the train was at the station in Indianapolis. He arose to go. I said: "You are a funny man."

"Why so?" he said, with a show of anger.

I said: "On this train you have gagged on a rib and have swallowed a live monkey, head, hair, tail, and all."

I don't know if my words were received as wisdom or nonsense. But I hope I planted in his mind the truth that every believer is a priest unto God and can go directly to God. The priesthood of all believers, not the priesthood of a class, needs to be taught and preached today—and believed.

* * *

Once—years ago—I went by train from New Orleans to Los Angeles. It was a tedious and tiresome trip. I got tired of reading and writing and looking out the car window. I wanted to do something to make the boredom less boresome and the travel less tiresome. So I decided to go through the car and ask this question of each passenger: "Have you prayed today?"

The first one I accosted was a big fat man in the smoking room of the car. That was the day when they had a separate room for smokers.

I said to the big fat man who was smoking a big fat cigar, "Excuse me, sir, but have you prayed today?" He greeted me in a voice that was half a grunt and half a snarl and informed me that was none of my business.

I got a polite no from a few passengers. I came to a seat where there were three young women—college students, judging from the college pennants on display. With courtesy in my approach, I said: "Excuse me, young ladies, but have you prayed today?" All three looked at me, but only one spoke. She told me that she "believed in religious matters but did not believe in making a public display of it."

The other young women only smiled at me, as though they were thinking that I had "vacant rooms for rent upstairs."

Having interviewed quite a number of passengers, I came to the twelfth-one to whom I asked the question. She was a little lady about seventy years old—or so I judged. She had on a little half-way bonnet and was neat and prim in her attire. Kindly and courteously, I said: "Excuse me, little lady, but have you prayed today?"

Her eyes flashed fire. She looked at me as though she pitied me for lack of mental ability and said, anger in her words: "My mother taught me never to talk to strangers when I travelled!"

The last of all the nineteen passengers I interviewed was a handsome man, with a minister's garb and appearance. I said: "Excuse me, sir, have you prayed today?"

"Yes, God bless you, sir. Have you?" I found out that he was a Methodist minister. I found out, too, that only one of those to whom I asked my question admitted that they had prayed or seem to want to make any remarks about prayer.

I suppose that in religious matters they had never come to believe that nothing lies beyond the reach of prayer except that which lies beyond the will of God.

Maybe they had never prayed often or for a long time. Maybe they had never had answers to their prayers—*if* they ever prayed.

13.
The Realization of a Dream

My father, a Baptist deacon for forty-two years, once remarked that his son, Bob, took to Baptist gatherings like a frog takes to a pond or a cat to a plate of milk.

From my boyhood days until now in my old age, I have enjoyed Baptist gatherings—whether the gathering was just a few neighbors in a country house, congregations in country churches, bigger congregations in large city churches, and still larger gatherings of multitudes in big city halls or outdoor coliseums.

The first public speech I ever made to a Baptist congregation was at the old Flint Hill Baptist Church near Pineville, North Carolina, founded in 1792. This speech on "Good Habits" was made to a group of Sunday School workers.

All these years I have enjoyed attending the meetings of Baptist associations. The first one I attended was when my father, a delegate, took me along with him, to the meeting of the York County Baptist Association, meeting in York, when I was twelve years old and a three-month-old Christian. All the men who spoke stirred me, making me wonder if ever I should have the chance to speak to some gatherings.

There was one Vesuvius in eruption in my boyish bosom—the burning desire to be a preacher, for, from the day I was born again, I believed that God wanted to use me as a preacher of the gospel. I used to say this to myself: "Someday, maybe years from now, when you get an education, you will have the chance to speak to congregations as large as those of the York Baptist Association." Years later, my yearnings were satisfied, my prayers answered.

Incidentally, a big picture which I framed and put on the wall of my office has intensified my ambition to be a preacher to whom people could listen without being apathetically bored. The picture is of Cicero in his speech against Cataline before the Roman Senate. Cicero verbally painted Cataline so "monstrously evil" that the Roman senators crowded to one side of the Senate chamber and left Cataline all by himself on the other side of the Senate chamber, acting toward Cataline as though to be near him would be near a plague.

I had, since twelve years of age, wanted to preach. I have done much of it, though much of it might be classed by critics as mediocre rather than magnificent.

Without boasting I can say what Samuel Rutherford once said: "Next to loving Christ himself, I love the preaching of Christ more than anything in this world." If I have ever poorly preached Christ, it is not because I love him poorly! I love Christ Jesus more than anyone whose name I have ever heard—more than anyone whom I have ever known.

For years I have preached him as Heaven's Bread for earth's hunger, Heaven's Water for earth's thirst, Heaven's Light for earth's darkness, Heaven's Love for earth's hate, Heaven's Wisdom for earth's folly, Heaven's Beauty for earth's ugliness, Heaven's Grace for earth's guilt, Heaven's Joy for earth's sorrows, Heaven's Glory for earth's shame, Heaven's Peace for earth's strife, Heaven's Justification for earth's condemnation, Heaven's Salvation for earth's damnation, Heaven's Life for earth's death.

I can say of myself what Samuel Chadwick said as to himself: "I would rather pay to preach than to be paid not to preach. Preaching has its price in agony of sweat and tears. No calling has such heartbreak, but preaching is a calling an archangel might covet. I thank God that by his grace he called me into the ministry of preaching."

I believe God called me to preach the Word (2 Tim. 4:2). And I rejoice in what E. C. Sheahan wrote:

Whether the opportunity seems to be favorable or unfavorable, whether it is convenient or inconvenient, whether it is welcome or unwelcome, you as a preacher of the Word are to show people in what way their lives are wrong and convince them—rebuking and correcting, warning and urging and encouraging them, being unflagging and inexhaustible in patience and teaching.

Having no doubt as to my conversion, knowing that I am saved by the grace of God through repentance toward God and faith in the Savior, I agree with what Spurgeon said: "How possible to be a preacher of the gospel and yet to be unconverted."

I have preached on all sorts of subjects—some unusual, such as: "Jewels in a Hog's Snout," (Prov. 11:22); "Chasing Fleas and Dead Dogs" (1 Sam. 24:14; 26:20); "A Smoked Bottle" (Ps. 119:83); "Feet to Fathoms" (Acts 27:28); "Treasures of the Snow" (Job 38:22).

Hundreds of subjects I have used, but in all sermons, Jesus was the Person presented and proclaimed. To take Jesus out of a sermon is like taking heat out of fire, melody out of music, numbers out of mathematics, fact out of history, fiction out of literature, brains out of the skull and expecting intelligence, and blood out of the body and expecting health.

I have preached in small country and town church houses with a membership of less than one hundred, in school houses where people wanted "church services," in small thatched-hut churches in the jungle, in big church houses in big cities with memberships into the thousands. I have preached to large congregations at Bellevue (which had ninety-two hundred members when I resigned). I have preached in state capitol buildings to the assembled members of the legislature.

One night I preached in the Constitutional Hall in Washington, D.C., after the Westminister Choir had given a concert.

I have preached in scores of colleges and universities in many states, north and south, east and west. I have preached at picnics and in cemeteries on memorial days.

I have preached in Mexico, in Japan, in Korea, in Turkey, in Nazareth, Israel, in Jerusalem, in Cana of Galilee (where Bellevue Church, through Dr. Burkle, built a Baptist Chapel), in France, in England, in India, in Moscow, Russia, in Egypt, in Italy, and in every state in the United States except Utah and Nevada. I have preached in Bible conferences of all denominations and in interdenominational youth camps.

My hope, as a boy, that when I became a man and a preacher God would see to it that I spoke to many people became not a dream, but a reality, not a hope but an actuality.

Four consecutive years I served as president of the Tennessee Baptist State Convention—and, at each convention, addressed many—preaching my sermon "A Greater Than Solomon" when the Convention met in Murfreesboro, Tennessee, in the 1930's.

I spoke to thousands when I gave the Convention sermon in New Orleans in 1929 using 1 Corinthians 15:3-4 as my text.

I spoke to thousands at Founders' Week of the Moody Bible Institute, when Dr. Grey was president.

I spoke to thousands in and around the Billy Sunday Tabernacle at Winona Lake Bible Conference, Winona Lake, Indiana.

I served three consecutive terms—1948-1951—as president of the great Southern Baptist Convention, greatest evangelical body on the face of the earth. I spoke to thousands during those three years, in my president's address and on other programs connected with the Southern Baptist Convention.

Two events during my first term as president took place in 1949, when the Southern Baptist Convention met in Oklahoma City. Those two events continue to live in my mind and heart, and, I think, in the minds and hearts of many who were present that May day, 1949.

The Aldredge Amendment was put before the Convention. This amendment was a threat to the harmony of the Convention. This amendment stated that "no one who belongs to or is affiliated with any state or local council of churches connected with the Federal Council of Churches shall be eligible to serve on any board, agency, or institution of the Convention either as an official or board member."

Many were clamoring for the adoption of this amendment. I believed the statement of the Aldredge Amendment if adopted would do evil and not good in the Convention. I handed the gavel to the first vice-president, Dr. Porter Bailes, pastor of the First Baptist Church, Tyler, Texas, and made this statement: "Brethren, I think most of you know my position is not favorable to the Federal Council of Churches. But this amendment is a mistake. And I make the motion that it be tabled."

Much to my relief, the Convention voted overwhelmingly to do so. John J. Hurt, editor of *The Baptist Standard* wrote me these words about those two events: "I remember both events quite well. . . . You saved the Convention from a major split."

Number two: Dr. E. W. Perry, a noted Negro minister, pastor of the Tabernacle Baptist Church in Oklahoma City and vice-president of the National Baptist Convention, U.S.A. was scheduled to preach.

Tall, dignified, earnest, Dr. Perry turned to me before he preached his sermon, and said: "Mr. President, I have been more than sixty years coming from a log cabin in Mississippi where I was born to the high place to which my people have elected me. I ask you in advance, please don't ring me down."

I promised him I would not. Then, for an hour, Dr. Perry held the audience in his grasp, with a sermon which all called "great" as, with intensity, he preached the gospel.

When Dr. Perry concluded his sermon and had seated himself, I arose and said: "Dr. Perry, come here and stand by me and take my hand. I want this Convention to witness a parable in black and white, written in red. Over sixty years ago, you were born in a log cabin in Mississippi. I, too, was born in a log cabin in South Carolina.

"You and I have been placed in the high positions we occupy by the vote of confidence of our people. But the same Christ who saved you is the Christ who saved me, and both of us have been washed white in the precious blood of the Lamb. This is the parable in black and white written in red."

Of this event, Dr. O. W. Taylor, editor of *The Baptist and Reflector,* wrote: "That accomplished more for good race relations than all the academic theorizing in the world."

I am not throwing any flowers at myself—I am just sharing gratefully how God granted the desire of my heart as a youth "to preach sometime when I became a preacher" to some large congregations.

If I had one hundred heads and each head had one hundred mouths and each mouth had ten tongues and each tongue should talk one hundred minutes, I could hardly express the full measure of the gratitude of my heart for all that God has done for me!

61801

DATE DUE